The Mothers of Reinvention

The Mothers *of* Reinvention

Reclaim Your Identity,
Unleash Your Potential,
Love Your Life

BY

Jennifer Pate and Barbara Machen,

CREATORS AND HOSTS OF THE AWARD-WINNING WEB SERIES,
JEN AND BARB: MOM LIFE

Vanguard Press
A Member of the Perseus Books Group

Published by Vanguard Press
A Member of the Perseus Books Group

Designed by Trish Wilkinson
Set in 12 point Goudy Old Style

Library of Congress Cataloging-in-Publication Data

Pate, Jennifer.
    The mothers of reinvention : reclaim your identity, unleash your potential, love
your life / Jennifer Pate and Barbara Machen.
        p. cm.
    ISBN 978-1-59315-683-1 (pbk. : alk. paper)—ISBN 978-1-59315-693-0 (e-book)
1. Self-actualization (Psychology) in women. 2. Mothers—Psychology.
3. Women—Psychology. 4. Change (Psychology) I. Machen, Barbara. II. Title.
BF637.S4P37 2011
155.6'463—dc23
2011037225

Vanguard Press books are available at special discounts for bulk
purchases in the U.S. by corporations, institutions, and other organizations.
For more information, please contact the Special Markets Department at the
Perseus Books Group, 2300 Chestnut Street, Suite 200, Philadelphia, PA 19103,
or call (800) 810-4145, ext. 5000, or e-mail special.markets@perseusbooks.com.

10 9 8 7 6 5 4 3 2 1

For Jonas, my love for you is profound and eternal. I won life's lottery to have you as my partner and the father of my children. You are my inspiration.

For Cooper and Lilah, the two of you give me purpose and help keep everything in perspective.

And for my nephew, Kal-El. Your short life was full of big laughs. I miss you.

Mom, thank-you for showing me that there are so many other colors in the world besides the primary ones. It is that kind of thinking "outside the box" that has helped me in every area of my life.

Dad, you have always believed in me and taught me to find the beauty in nature, especially flowers. I love you.

My entire family (both born into and married into), your love and support mean more to me than you can ever imagine.

Barb, from meeting in a Mommy and Me class to becoming business partners, our friendship is deep and everlasting. You have taught me to believe in myself and stand firmly on my own two feet. I love you.

Jen

For my beautiful daughters, India and Soraya. I thank God every day for sending you to me. You are truly my angels, and you inspire me daily to be the best person I can be.

For my Handsome Prince. Thank you for always believing in me and for always saying "yes." You are a true partner and the love of my life.

To my mom and auntie for being the best role models any woman (girl) could have and for giving me the "gift" of confidence. To my mother-in-law Mercedeh for all the babysitting. Your are an important part of "my village."

Barb

When you recover or discover something that nourishes your soul and brings joy, care enough about yourself to make room for it in your life.

—Jean Shinoda Bolen

Contents

Acknowledgments

We are forever grateful to all the amazing moms who have shared their stories with us over the past few years. You may not realize it when you tell your story, but it helps make other women feel they are not alone on their journey.

A special thank-you to Danny Fishman. You believed in our vision when it was just an idea we were discussing, and without your persistence and dedication, we would not be where we are today.

Julie Hermelin, our friend and original director, you helped shape our show and gave tirelessly of your time, ideas, and direction. Your voice and energy live in *Mom Life*.

Our deepest appreciation to all of the amazing guests who shared their insights and information. You have helped us in our own lives and gave invaluable information to the millions of women who watch our show.

Our amazing producer with Specific Media, Samantha Giberga, you are the glue that holds us together. To watch you go from woman to mother (twice!) in our time with you has been beautiful.

Chris Sliney at Playground, for taking a crazy mom's call on your vacation and making the impossible happen.

A big thank-you to Brad Roth and Mark Feldstein at Stun Creative. You stuck with us and helped us turn our vision into a show. It has been and continues to be a pleasure to work with you and your team.

A special shout out to Jill Reisman at Stun. You keep this ship on course even in the choppiest of waters!

Our director and editor extraordinaire, Andrew Karlsruher, aka Young Andrew, you are a "Rock Star," and we are lucky to have you. You have helped elevate *Mom Life* to new heights. We thank you for that and for putting up with us and picking up the phone at all hours of the night when we called.

We would not have reached the millions of people without our partnership with Specific Media and the support of all of our sponsors over the last few years. Thank-you for understanding the importance of the power of moms and being committed to bringing them content that is important and relevant.

Dr. Phil, that day that we spent with you in your office and on your set was invaluable. You shared your wisdom and inspired us. A day with you was like getting a master's degree from Harvard!

To one of our biggest supporters, Abra Potkin. You have believed in us from the get-go and have been an important part of our journey.

Rachael Ray and her amazing team, we love being part of your community and being your "online moms." We appreciate your support of the importance of the "mom" conversation.

Rebecca Raphael, that week we spent together in LA getting all our stories down on paper was an invaluable contribution to this book.

Joel Gotler, our agent, we called you for some friendly advice, and you turned it into a book deal within days. You thought we had a voice that should be heard, and if it were not for you, this book might not have a publisher.

Larry Kirshbaum, our book agent, thank-you for holding our hands through the publishing process. Your enthusiasm gave us great confidence.

Roger Cooper and Vanguard Press, especially Georgina Levitt, working with you on this book has been a pleasure. We won the lottery with you and your team.

This book would be a box of ideas and thoughts if not for the amazing work of Francine LaSala. We will never forget the night we were holed up all night in a New York hotel room working with you. Your voice lives in this book.

The fresh eyes of Monica Harris, our editor, helped us get over the final hurdles to getting our message across.

Last, but not least, thank-you to all the viewers who take the time to watch our show and share your thoughts, and who have become part of our "village."

With love and gratitude,

Jen and Barb

Introduction

I Have What I Thought I Always Wanted;
Why Aren't I Happy?

If you picked up this book, you're probably feeling displaced and isolated in your role as both "mother" and "woman." You're feeling uncertain about what your real place in life is, and think that there's probably something wrong with you because you have everything you ever thought you wanted, *but there's still something missing*. Don't worry. You're not alone.

Barb

I have wanted three things out of life since I was a little girl. I wanted to be a talk show host, because I love talking to people and hearing their stories. I wanted to be financially secure, because growing up in a single-parent household, I never was. And I wanted a family with the best dad in the world for my kids. My dad was a substance abuser, and my parents divorced when I was young. Those circumstances gave me the "no-excuses" attitude I've brought to everything I do. I'm goal oriented, and I work hard at everything I do. I was president of my high school, was editor of the school newspaper, and received a scholarship to USC. I felt I could do anything I wanted. I was the girl soaring against the odds, and I had everything under control. What was most shocking to me about becoming a mom, however, was that none of the tricks I had used in my life seemed to work. Once my kids came along, it was like my "magic" was gone.

Jen

I always wanted happiness and a family. Along the way I had a love for dance and a desire to be a good businesswoman, but at the core of it all was family. I think that's why I was so confused when I had my husband and two children but still felt something was missing. I didn't realize how important the "me" was in my equation of happiness. I may be slightly old-fashioned in this respect, as many of my peers knew they wanted a huge career or to make a ton of money, but somewhere along the way, I grew to have my own desires and ambitions and didn't realize that was going to be a critical part of my family life.

The clear-cut, defined roles of motherhood of the June Cleaver era are now long gone, and the challenges that this generation of mothers are confronted with are brand new. We are post-feminism, post-Steinem. Women are more educated and better paid than ever before. We are CEOs and heads of state. We are getting married later and having children later still. And with all the value society places on independence and individuality, we are often confused about how to maintain our hard-won independence and individuality in the face of motherhood and domestic life. "You're just a mom" is a common observation even from other moms. It used to be that homemaker was a well-respected position in society, but that doesn't seem to be the case anymore. Listen and you'll hear women all the time saying things like they don't feel they have the right to spend money on themselves if they are not "working" or bringing money into the family. Whatever we do, for some reason we just don't feel it's good enough.

Whether we put expectations on ourselves or society imposes them on us, the end result is that modern women feel as though we are expected to be great mothers, loving wives, successful professionals, and superb homemakers, and we are also expected to look amazing, stay fit, and still have energy to have sex. Common sense tells us that being all of this at once is unrealistic. No one can live up to those expectations, and no one does. However, we try. When we can't do it, we somehow feel that we've failed. Marriage and kids affect every aspect of our lives, yet somehow we are surprised by just how much of a ripple effect our families have on our lives. We all dreamed the "fairy tale." We all had the fantasy that once we found our "prince" and had kids, our lives would be complete.

But real life is just that: *real*. There are ups and downs. There are amazing moments when you feel love beyond what you ever imagined could be possible to feel for another human being. And then there are the other moments, the "dark moments," when your kids won't stop whining, or you're picking up your spouse's dirty laundry off the floor for the umpteenth time, or you're having a difficult time paying the bills. Real life is not a fairy tale. Real life is monotonous . At the end of the day, it doesn't usually feel like a "happily ever after"—more like a reality show where they have to call in a British nanny. Here's the most important thing we have learned over the course of our own reinventions: **The more satisfied you are with yourself, the better you can deal with the chaos that surrounds you!** Reinvention is about finding a way to make everything come together. To find yourself, your soul, and nurture and love that part of you as much as you nurture and love those who count on you. It's a way to find joy and pleasure in your daily life, and that joy or pleasure can come in many forms— different for every person.

Reinvention *isn't* about balance. Balance is a nearly impossible concept that stresses one more than it helps. We've learned there is no defined equation you can fall back on, quantifying all the many elements of your life to make sure everything is even. That's not realistic.

Barb

For example, I was dealing with work and kids and marriage and try- ing to "balance" it all. I was working hard at everything all the time and feeling that I was succeeding at nothing. I used to think my hus- band was the problem, that if I could control him more, things would fall into place better. Now I realize that my unhappiness had nothing to do with him—it had to do with thinking I had to get it all in balance. Meanwhile, I didn't even know what "it all" was.

Betty Friedan's *The Feminine Mystique* (1963) sparked a na- tional debate about women's roles. In the book, Friedan defines women's unhappiness as "the problem that has no name." She pins the blame on an idealized image of femininity that she calls "the feminine mystique," theorizing that this mystique denies women the opportunity to develop their own identities, which can ultimately lead to problems for women and their families. And that's what we're really getting at here. That's why reinven- tion is so important for women.

So no, reinvention is not about balance. Rather, it's about per- sonal validation and rediscovering yourself to make you feel hap- pier and more satisfied about your place within your family. It's about taking the mystery out of the mystique. It's about getting your piece of the pie in your family. It doesn't have to be a big piece, but it has to be something. The validation you crave has to come from within, through fulfillment. Without fulfillment, there can't be joy, and without joy in what we're doing, everything falls apart.

But with so many expectations of us, how can we possibly have time to figure out what gives us fulfillment beyond our family life, let alone make it happen? Even the most accomplished women with families can feel something is missing from their lives. But how do we figure out what that is and actually get it? How do we get that extra slice that makes life not just something we have been given and must maintain, but something we, in our souls, feel is worth living beyond the mother role?

Jen

I didn't know what it was I wanted. This was my biggest challenge, because I only knew I needed *something*. My reinvention was an evolution. As mothers, that's how it happens for most of us. When Elizabeth Gilbert, author of *Eat, Pray, Love*, felt lost in her life, she checked out and traveled around the world for a year to find herself. Once you're a mom, that's simply not an option. So what can you do? How can you find and do what will make you feel complete as a person while managing everything else you have going on—whether it's starting a new business, taking a class, losing the baby weight, or finding a way to spend more time with your kids? Whatever it is, you have to find it, and you have to do it *now*.

This book is for women who feel they're on a treadmill of life. It's for stay-at-home moms who feel over- and underwhelmed, for working mothers who feel the strain of living dual lives, and for single mothers who are navigating parenthood on their own. No matter which describes you, you need something that fulfills you outside your traditional roles and obligations.

Just a few years ago, we were both in the same place you are now. We had everything we had dreamed of—the husband, the house, the kids. But something was still *missing*. We couldn't put our finger on what the void was, but it left us questioning ourselves and feeling guilty and confused. We hadn't met each other yet, so we each felt isolated as we searched for help navigating this uncertain time in our lives and tried to figure out if something was "wrong" with us. For us, the missing piece came into place when we met at a Mommy & Me class. At first glance, each of us thought the other had it totally together. As our friendship grew, we discovered that we both felt unsure of our ability to be good moms, were concerned about the toll our children had taken on our marriages, and were confused about our own identities.

Concerned we were off the path, yet still wanting our ideal life, we started sharing our ideas of what our perfect life would look like. Little did we know that with that sharing and trying to work things out together, our reinvention had already begun. Since we started our show, *Jen and Barb: Mom Life*, the biggest question women have asked us is, "How did you guys do that?" The subtext here has not been about the details of producing a show, but rather about how we managed to make such a big shift in our lives, especially given our roles as mothers, wives, and career women. Long story short, we worked at it, and worked at it hard, and we did it. And now we're going to show you how. Yes, you'll still want to scream at your kids and your husband from time to time, but when you feel fulfilled within yourself, you'll have better perspective. You won't be focused on the petty things as often. You'll be able to see the big picture much more clearly. You'll be able to put your energies into the things that matter most and let the rest roll off your back.

You set the tone for your entire family. If Mom isn't happy, nobody is happy. Feeling fulfilled is something that no one can take away from you. It is yours and yours alone, and it is an essential part of your happiness, your well-being, and the well-being of your family. So it is you who we are talking to. Do not feel guilty that your family does not fully complete you. It's okay to want something for yourself. It's not a luxury, it's a necessity, and throughout this book, we'll show you why it's a necessity. And the time for it is now.

Whether you're a new mom whose world has just been rocked in ways you couldn't ever have envisioned or an empty nester who's ready to start a new chapter, whether you're struggling to figure out the origin of your void or are crystal clear on what's missing in your life and are just looking for a way to make change happen, we want to help you spark your reinvention and start living to your full potential as a mom and a woman.

We wrote this book because we got tired of all the bitching we encountered, in blogs and magazine columns, about how difficult and aggravating motherhood can be, but no one was offering solutions. We craved a way to improve our situations, and we couldn't find one. We searched in bookstores, we turned to daytime television, and we couldn't find it. Many of the books and websites were whining and complaining, and none offered solutions or answers. There was very little "conversation" going on. Everything we found was about what was "right" or "wrong," and the way we "should" be doing things. Most materials were geared toward "how to" or parenting and motherhood—not the emotional aspects. This is where our reinvention began.

Passionate to find solutions to navigating modern motherhood, we created *Mom Life*, an award-winning web series. We wanted to take the intimate conversations that moms were having and open them to a larger forum of sharing and finding solutions.

And now we're taking the next step: We're actually mapping out how we and other moms have reinvented, to help you plan your own reinvention. One dictionary defines reinvention this way: "To invent again or anew, especially without knowing that the invention already exists." Think about it. You already have it within you; now is the time to access it.

This book is a guide to help you find the answers for YOU. Not your neighbor, not your sister, but YOU. Everyone's reinvention looks different. We will take you through the steps we walked to help you discover what you want and navigate the changes with your partner, your children, and everyone in your life. We'll share our personal journeys of reinvention as well as motivational stories from other women to remind you that you are not alone and can ultimately get that little piece of the pie that will offer you the validation you so richly deserve.

For all the women featured in this book, each of our reinventions happened for different reasons and at different times, and each of us has something to teach you if you are ready to learn. In addition to targeted advice from experts we've had on our show, *The Mothers of Reinvention* also features women of all ages who have reinvented in new careers or have created sidelines that work around their kids' schedules. Some are relatively new moms, others are empty nesters navigating through new freedoms and the new world of becoming a grandparent.

Whatever the case may be, these women, like us, and soon like you, knew a change was needed. They knew they needed that "something else" to complete them, and amazingly, they all took relatively the same steps to get what they needed. *The Mothers of Reinvention* outlines those steps for you, giving you the tools you need to begin and complete your reinvention. You'll clearly see what's causing the "void" in you and use the tools we share to work your way to fulfillment, working with yourself, your partner, your children, and your village. And here's the really good news:

Reinvention isn't something you do once and it's done. As long as you live and your life continues to change, you can enjoy rediscovering yourself and what fulfills you every step of the way by using the advice and tools you'll find here.

If you're ready to stop bitching and start acting, you're ready to reinvent. You're ready to finally take that step to reclaim your identity, unleash your potential, and truly start enjoying your life. If you're ready to claim your slice of the pie by rediscovering yourself, then you're ready to reinvent.

Welcome to *The Mothers of Reinvention*. It's time for you to realize your full potential as a woman while still maintaining your joy as a mom and/or wife. Just by reading this introduction, your reinvention has already begun.

Chapter 1

Reinvent Your Perception
Putting the Pep Back in Your Step

I had always wanted to have children so badly, to be "the head of the little people." My husband and I worked tirelessly for me to get pregnant for a year and a half. Finally we had succeeded, and with twins.

I imagined that now my life would be complete—that I had realized my ultimate dream with a husband and kids. A family. I thought that it would be easy and joyful to raise my two girls. Why wouldn't it be? I was a smart, educated, organized woman. I had managed employees and navigated myself through very challenging obstacles in both my personal and professional lives with a smile on my face. I wasn't a pregnant teen having a baby by surprise. I was a thirty-five-year-old woman who had made a calculated decision about having children, and I was prepared and ready to slide right into that new role.

I had been home with my new twins for about three days when I started to feel the walls closing in on me. I couldn't breast-feed; they were crying nonstop. I hadn't showered or slept for days. I began to feel trapped, claustrophobic, like someone had a noose around my neck and was pulling it just tight enough for me to be in a constant state of pain. I remember turning to my husband one night in bed and saying,

"You can keep these kids and the house, but I can't stay here; I won't make it."

I felt so inadequate. I had "performed" my life "really well" before this family came along. Now the feeling that I was a failure had completely consumed me. And I felt so guilty for feeling like I did.

—Barb

I thought that being the best possible mother and wife would ultimately make my kids the happiest, most well-adjusted people ever, and that I would have the marriage that legends are made of! This was a direct result of my parents' divorce. I was brought up to believe that family was the most important thing. Period. Full stop. I grew up around aunts, uncles, cousins, and grandparents. I was also lucky to have one sister and two brothers. My parents ultimately divorced when I was a teenager, and it was like someone pulled the rug out from underneath me, as if everything I was ever told or taught to believe wasn't true anymore. The idea that my parents couldn't work it out and had a difficult divorce made me feel hopeless for awhile.

I decided a long time ago that when or if I got married, it was going to be the best and happiest marriage, and that my children were going to know that they were the luckiest children alive. So I quit working and dove into being a stay-at-home mom with full force. I traveled around the world with two children in diapers to be with my husband for his work. We even relocated to North Carolina for a year for his work when they were two and three years old.

It was at a party during our year away that I realized I was losing myself, and that really confused me. The party consisted of all the people my husband was working with: the cast and crew of the TV show he was producing. They all had these inside jokes and were enjoying the creative process of what they were doing. I kept referring to anecdotes from when I was a casting director or a dancer. This made me feel irrelevant. Was nothing that I was currently doing interesting enough to talk about in a social setting? Did I have anything left other than talk about parenting and housekeeping? Who had I become? I felt really bad about myself and in-credibly guilty for having these feelings. How could I have something for myself and still be the wife and mother I want to be for my family?

—Jen

Haven't we all been there at one time or another? Haven't we just wanted to get up and leave the chaos and incessant demands of motherhood behind? Haven't we found ourselves in heated, intense arguments over his-and-her interpretations of reality? And haven't we all romanticized the days when we only had ourselves to worry about—or even just ourselves and our husbands? When dinner wasn't something you necessarily planned, unless you planned to go out someplace special, and then needed to plan to buy yourself a nice new dress or a pair of pretty shoes just for that occasion?

Nothing that happens before the children come along pre-pares you for how drastically your life is going to change. Sure, people can tell you it's tough, but you may tell yourself that those people are soft, that you'll be a much better mother than they are! Your know what to do—you've read all the books! And why wouldn't you have thought that way? You were totally set up for that, weren't you?

When you first learned you were pregnant, your life was a whirl-wind of well wishes. People smiled at you and your ever-growing bump when you passed them in the street. Strangers wanted to touch you all the time. You were the most important person in the lives of the older women in your family; droves of long-forgotten aunts and friends of the family popped out of the woodwork to give you advice and little stuffed bears and improbably small booties. People wanted to know how you were feeling—if you were sleep-ing okay and if there was anything special they could treat you to, like the ice cream you were always craving. You received your "This Week Your Baby Is . . . " e-mails, and everyone was so excited to hear that the fetus was the size of a blueberry! A string bean! A spatula!

Showers were thrown in your honor. Gifts showed up on your doorstep all the time, gifts addressed to you! It was just like the months that led up to your wedding, with so many people excited about you and your good news. But unlike then, when you were a bride to be and had a gown to consider squeezing into, you could eat practically anything you wanted. You were encouraged to never skip the whipped cream.

You went for sonograms, and everyone wanted to see your pictures. And people wanted to take pictures of you all the time. Except as your bump grew, you couldn't help but notice how more and more, part of your face or your whole head would be cut out of the picture. . . . (You chalked it up to excitement, of course.)

You read all the books, your partner and you both. You knew exactly what to expect when you were expecting. Of course you did! You took birthing classes and made decisions together. And you and your partner were on the same page about everything— or just about everything. You were over the moon that you had chosen such a smart and sensitive partner, someone with whom you rarely fought!

Then the big day came. Hospital workers and family members doted on you, making you comfortable for the big event. Everyone was concerned with you having enough rest. And you had no idea that the night before this day was the last night you were ever going to sleep well, perhaps for the remainder of your adult life.

Maybe you had a tough labor and delivery. Maybe you struggled with breast-feeding and couldn't get the baby to latch on properly. Or maybe you had opted not to breast-feed and were then harassed for the remainder of your hospital stay to reconsider by an endless parade of night nurses and lactation specialists. Going home would be a relief.

From the minute you brought your beautiful, perfect pieces of swaddled snuggles home, your home was turned upside down. You were still uncomfortable from birth and trying to recover, but you had to get up every hour to tend to the baby's needs. Maybe your partner helped sometimes; maybe he didn't hear all the small cries you did. Maybe after awhile he stopped hearing them altogether in the middle of the night. Soon the sleep deprivation, the incessant needs of your little one, and the constant onslaught of interlopers coming to help out/interfere had become too much. You may have felt rage like never before. Plus that partner you thought you had chosen so well all of a sudden became the scourge of the earth, and you fought almost constantly.

If you're reading this book, you have been there. You have made that transition from what you thought was your fantasy to reality. Save for the special moments of pure, luscious joy you can only derive from the little one or little ones you brought into your life, you've come to see that the reality of motherhood, with its constant demands and worries and stresses, isn't quite what you had imagined it would be. If you're reading this book, you have been just where Barb was with those babies, so small and so demanding, feeling helpless and inadequate and tired and frustrated beyond imagination—perceiving that I would be "head of the little people" and not being in charge or control of anything.

If you're reading this book, you have been just where Jen was, for whom just having a baby and experiencing motherhood meant so much; it didn't occur to her that there would be something missing in it for her.

Of course, it isn't our fault. Step back and think about it, and you can see how you came by the perceptions that tripped you up when you became a mother. But the problem goes back much further than the first announcement you made that a baby was on the way.

As little girls, we grow up with the whole princess theory: that we're going to find our prince charming and build this amazing life together, and of course we're going to be happy all the time. We imagine what our weddings will be like and romanticize having babies, pushing our plastic dollies around in their strollers, feeding them, diapering them, dressing them up in adorable little clothes, and of course just dropping them when we find something else we want to play with.

As we grow up, we may stop playing with baby dolls, but we start to babysit, and we always try to be nicer and more fun with the kids than their mother seems to be to them. . . . By the time we get to college, we start looking at the boys we date a little differently; we start to wonder if our boyfriends will indeed become our husbands, and for many of us, we can't get to that point fast enough. Every girl has in her head what her wedding will look like and what her ring will look like. Many actually think about the husband last.

Barb

I picked out a wedding ring before I found a husband. I didn't even have a boyfriend, and I knew what ring I wanted.

Then we finally find "the one"; we anxiously await "the ring" at every holiday or special occasion. We can't wait to begin our lives!

You spend your whole life chasing a fantasy, and then you have your big fantasy wedding (check!), and maybe you have your honeymoon (check!), and you don't feel 100 percent happiness or fulfillment yet because you rationalize: Once I have my kids (once the fantasy is complete), I will truly be happy.

And if you're reading this book, you know that isn't exactly true. You get to the point where you complete your checklist and then: the letdown. You have everything you ever wanted, but instead of a glowing sense of contentment shining within you, there's a mysterious void. This void can show up at any point after you start having children. It may be right after you have your first baby or when your kids are going to college, but trust us, it will come. You have this perfect construct of a life built around you, but there's a part missing—and that part is you. Not your presence or your efforts, but *you*. You the person. You, whoever you are, whatever your identity is apart from being a mother and wife.

There is much self-sacrifice when you have a family. How could you not lose yourself in it? Where's your sense of self-worth when you work tirelessly to satisfy every need your children have, with very little reward or even a small sense of appreciation? Is this the fairy tale you thought it was going to be? Is this what "happily ever after" really means? Cinderella indeed. (Except you can forget about the party dress and the heels for now.)

"Who am I in this new life?" you may be wondering. We suppose we know how we got here, but we often think, how long do I have to stay? There is a way to stay and truly enjoy this new life, but you need to do some work to get yourself to the place where that's true.

BLOCK THE NOISE

This advice is for new moms especially, but we all fall into this trap at some point or another, no matter how seasoned we are. Here's the first way we're going to advise you to start feeling better about yourself and your situation: Stop reading every little piece of parenting literature you can get your hands on. Stop obsessing over the mixed messages books, magazines, and media feed you. You read and you read and you read, and you get confused because there are

Barb

I felt like I didn't know anything about parenting because I read everything. All that information wasn't helping me. It was only making me feel less secure in my ability as a mom.

so many messages to absorb. And guess what: Most of them are irrelevant. In fact, most are designed to confuse you, to shock you, to disempower you.

New parents crave information. No matter who you are, what your education is, or what age you are, first-time parenthood comes as a shock; none of us knows what in the hell we are doing! Though this information can be helpful, don't doubt your instincts, and there is no better source of information than discussing what you are going through with another mom!

Jen

When my son was about nine months old, I found my husband noodling around on WebMD.com. He faced me, looking a little pale, and told me that he thought our son was a dwarf. Although Cooper was a bit premature and had a big noggin, there were no signs that anything was wrong with this kid. I looked at the worry in my husband's eyes, and I laughed. You can only imagine the anger that invoked in him, but I couldn't stop laughing. First of all, Cooper wasn't a dwarf, but even if he was, there wasn't anything we could do about it but love our son. The point of this story is not that I am insensitive to my husband's concerns, but that sometimes there is a bit too much information out there, and it can mislead you. Instead of researching all that could be wrong with your child, actually spend that time with your child, and you'll see more clearly that most likely everything is fine.

REINVENT YOUR PERCEPTION:
BE SELECTIVE ABOUT WHAT YOU READ

The mother-to-be enters the baby store without a clue and leaves with an obscene new credit card balance and a trunkload of gadgets and devices and thousands of tiny outfits that will probably never be worn. She reads articles about every possible thing that can go wrong with a fetus as it develops. She watches melodramatic TV shows about "real births" and worries about how it's all going to turn out. When everything turns out fine, she is harassed by lactation consultants, who pretty much assure her that her baby will die without breast milk. She worries about "nipple confusion." She examines every diaper for signs of something having gone terribly wrong because she once ate tuna sushi while she was pregnant, even though she had been advised against it.

Especially for new mothers, the pressure can be too intense if we let it be. Of course moms want the best for their children. Help is necessary. Unfortunately, other people always think they know what's best for your child, and they are not ashamed to push their advice on you. Do your best to sift through it. There is a lot of information out there. Some may be very helpful, but some may really confuse you as well. Go back to your gut! You're the mom, don't forget that.

LOOK AFTER YOU, TOO

There are two important ways that women tell themselves they are good mothers. One of these is their ability to calm and sooth their babies crying, the other is their ability to breast feed. When one of those fails the feelings of inadequacy are incredible.

—Dr. Diana Barnes, expert on perinatal mood disorders

We are trained as women to "suck it up" and "deal with it," but it's really important that if we're having a tough time with parenting, we open up. Having children changes everything. The first few months of motherhood are especially tough, and four out of five women may experience something called "baby blues" to some extent. A change in life, constant demands, sleep deprivation—they're all bound to take their toll no matter how much you love that baby.

"New motherhood is one of the most stressful and anxiety-producing times in the life of a family," says Dr. Diana Barnes. "I don't know of any other job where you're on call 24 hours a day, 7 days a week. Where you don't get to take a lunch break or go to the bathroom by yourself or get a paid vacation. It's a tough, tough job. You can love your baby and hate the job!"

With baby blues, you may feel some or all of the following symptoms, which generally go away in a matter of a few days:

- mood swings;
- anxiety;
- sadness;
- irritability;
- decreased concentration; and
- trouble sleeping.

However, if the symptoms go on longer and seem to get worse and not better, it could be postpartum depression (PPD). About 800,000 women each year experience PPD. Says Dr. Barnes, "The most common indicator of PPD is overwhelming anxiety; an overwhelming sense of paralysis triggered by a crying baby. Many women afflicted by PPD feel that their baby would be better off with another mother, that they're 'going through the motions'; that they're 'taking care of the baby but there is a wall. They feel emotionally disconnected.'" PPD symptoms include

- loss of appetite;
- insomnia;
- intense irritability and anger;
- exhaustion;
- loss of libido;

- feelings of shame, guilt, or inadequacy;
- severe mood swings;
- withdrawal from family and friends;
- difficulty bonding with the baby; and
- thoughts of harming yourself or the baby.

Getting early treatment for PPD can speed your recovery and get your life back on track.

"One of the things we don't recognize in our culture here is that new mothers need to be mothered," says Dr. Barnes. "You need to be taken care of first so that then you can go out there and be a nurturing mom."

This book is not about PPD, but we wanted to address it because it's important to realize that PPD exists and that it needs to be treated. Postpartum depression is a serious medical condition, not something that's going to be fixed by reinventing yourself, so if it seems like this is something that could be happening to you, please talk to your doctor and get the help you need.

WHAT'S YOUR VIEW?

Barb

It took me awhile to see what kind of mom I was in the beginning. I was so uptight. I thought everything had to be perfect. I always had my kids beautifully dressed in fancy clothes. Other moms would walk around in sweats with their kids in mismatched outfits, looking homeless. And here I was, always impeccably dressed, with toddlers running around in dry-clean-only clothes. Then one day I realized that those other women weren't crazy—I was. I stepped back and looked at myself and wondered who I was trying to be. Did I really believe that if I dressed the part, I would somehow be a better mom? Is that really how I saw things?

Reinvention happens in stages, and the first is in your *percep-tion* of things. You go around for a while thinking that things are a certain way, and then you start to see things with new eyes. You realize that something is not working, and you're not sure why. That you have everything you thought you ever wanted, and it's not lining up the right way. You're striving to find validation in your role as a mother, but you can't quite get there, and it's frustrating the hell out of you.

So here's the thing. You have to change your perception—and this is going to seem a little harsh, but it's essential to understand this before you move on to anything else.

Reinvent Your Perception: There Is No "Validation" in Motherhood Alone

We put "validation" in quotes because it isn't quite that cut and dry, but it is an important perception to grapple with. Validation is a big part of who we are as human beings, but it's not something we should be actively seeking as mothers. Yes, you can feel joy when you see your child do something you taught him. You can be relieved that he looked both ways before crossing the street and has a sense of keeping safe or be proud when you watch him walk down the aisle at his high school graduation. But none of this is really about you; it's about him. You molded the clay, but the clay was there. You helped the clay become something magical, but the magic was already inherent within. You don't make your children what they are; you bring it out in them.

Being honest with yourself and seeing things as they are is a very important step. It's almost impossible to find self-worth *solely* in being a mom, and honestly, you shouldn't be looking for it there anyway. You may be the center of the universe of your family, but that's just because you hold it together. It may be a difficult truth to face, but if you want your only validation as a human being to come from your role as a mother and/or wife, with nothing else to hang your hat on, you're going to be disappointed. Motherhood is an "invisible" job. Validation of who you are has to come from various places, not motherhood alone. You need to find yourself, *your real self*, within the context of your family.

We are in no way minimizing your role as a mother. It's the most important job anyone could ever have. All we're saying is that you need to have something beyond your role of mother, something you are *passionate* about, that you can unleash from within, that will bring you a sense of joy that's all your own.

MOTHER OF REINVENTION: MELISSA

Turning Anxiety into Creativity

MELISSA BURNETT, married ten years, two kids

BEST ADVICE: Listen *to your mind and your body. Stay open, and your mind and body will guide you.*

"I struggled quite a bit before finding clarity. I had everything I wanted . . . a healthy baby girl, the freedom to stay home, great husband, family, and friends! But I needed more. I wanted to feel productive, and I was not getting enough mental stimulation. I sort of lost myself.

"After trying many different things, I found that writing children's books and poetry made me the happiest. Even then, it took me a while to realize that this is what I am supposed to be doing.

"I started a project on my own and did not discuss it with anyone. Around that time we had a checkup with the pediatrician, at which I was told to get rid of the pacifier. This completely shook me up because I, at the time, was also addicted to the pacifier (my golden weapon to prevent tantrums, crying, keeping other objects out of her mouth, and mostly to help her sleep). The project I started was my book, *The Paci Fairy*.

"I was in love with my daughter and in love with being a mother and in love with the opportunity to stay home with her. I put several hours aside during the day (mostly her nap time) to focus on my project. My daughter inspired me to write and 'story-tell,' and she became my muse.

"I had the full support of my husband, who knows a happy woman makes a happy wife and mommy. He is a rare species. He not only works as a commercial broker, but he is hands on around the house, taking care of chores, cooking, and our daughter. He does everything from dishes to laundry and is the most wonderful father I could ever imagine for my daughter. As far as support, he is my biggest fan and allows me the respect and freedom to do as I wish with ideas and business ventures.

"What I can tell you is to have no regrets, no matter what your choices have been. Never regret anything, because everything that has happened up until this point has brought you here, reading this book. You must have faith. Explore, explore . . . . , explore, and *discover yourself*.

"We are all in this together. There is never a plateau to reach, just a moment to relish. There are no rules or laws, or right or wrong. You set your own standards and make your own choices. Take the risk, find the courage, and follow your bliss. In doing this, you should discover your light. Once you identify your light . . . , own it, trust it, and be true to it. . . . You will shine so bright that everything else will fall into place."

What we love about Melissa's story is that she turned what seemed a predicament on its head. Although she was anxious about get-

ting rid of the pacifier, both for her daughter and herself, she turned it into an opportunity for creativity and forged a path that was both unexpected and rewarding.

IT'S WHAT YOU SEE AND
WHAT YOU MAKE OF HOW YOU SEE IT

Typically, women in the early twenty-first century are getting married and having kids later, so we've already had some experience of life. We have a fully developed identity before we jump in to merge our lives with our husbands', and we have a fully developed sense of autonomy before we become mothers. We have careers and social lives and passions and interests. And when we reinvent ourselves, we have to remember all of these things.

Barb

I was a confident, super-positive, optimistic, "nothing is going to rain on my parade" woman. I thought the normal rules of life didn't apply to me, and in my mind things always worked out in my favor. When a boyfriend broke up with me, it was his loss. If I didn't get a job, then it wasn't really a job I wanted anyway, and the job I was going to get would be way better. I could always make things happen. I was in charge of my own destiny. When I became a mother, all of that changed.

Think about it this way: If you slept on the floor all your life, you wouldn't miss having a bed, because the floor would be all you ever knew. But if you have slept in a bed your whole life and now you're sleeping on the floor, well, that's a hard adjustment. When you didn't know what you were missing, it didn't matter. If you got married when you were eighteen and never lived on your own, you wouldn't notice that you can keep your house clean because there is no interference or clutter. But when you get married at thirty or later and merge households, you can't help but feel a sting of panic when you see somebody bringing his old, frayed Lazy Boy or drum set from college into your house. It's not wrong; that's just how it goes.

You used to be able to make decisions based solely on how they would affect you. You used to be focused on your place in life all the time, without thinking about it. Before you were a wife and mother, everything had to do with you.

Jen

Before I had children, I came and went as I pleased. If I felt like working out at 7:30 p.m. and then going to dinner with friends at 9:30 p.m., that's what I did. On the weekends I got up when I wanted, read the newspaper or a book if I felt like it, maybe met a friend for brunch, went to the beach to rollerblade or to a yoga class, hung out at a coffee shop, went home to relax, then went out with friends. Just writing that seems like I'm talking about someone else. Was that actually me?

One morning when Cooper was three months old, I ran out of coffee. Not a good thing for a sleep-deprived mother of a colicky baby (and don't any of you suggest he was colicky because I was drinking coffee!). The ordeal of putting the baby in his car seat, carrying it down the flight of stairs to my car, driving to Starbucks, getting the baby out of the car seat and into his stroller, getting the coffee, and reversing the whole scenario to get home was a nightmare! As he cried from the back seat on the way home, I cried in the front. Big change from my previous life.

It's not that you aren't happy being a wife and a mother. It's not that you don't find joy in nurturing your family. These things just aren't enough on their own. You think you have all the pieces to the puzzle, and you still feel a void. Fine. Actually, good. Because what you're craving is not a substitute or replacement for the life you have. **What you're craving is an enhancement, an addition. An icing you can put on an already delicious cake to make it that much better.** Now pat yourself on the back for even acknowledging that something's missing, and let's work together to figure out how to fill the void.

If you're a new mom, chances are that part of what's causing your feeling of emptiness is that you're in a state of shock. You had *perceptions* of what your reality was going to be, and your reality doesn't match up with the fairy tale. You feel trapped by the constant demands, when everything you've ever read tells you you're supposed to be "enjoying your new baby." But you aren't having such a good time, and you feel guilty because you're not. You feel like there's something wrong with you.

Indeed, it is one of the hardest things to imagine when you're in the throes of new motherhood that you're ever going to enter the world again as a normal person. With a nice, spit-up-free outfit and cute, non-sensible shoes. Or when you think you are out of the woods and finally going to get those eight hours of uninterrupted sleep, you are instead anxiously waiting for the sound of the car to drive up to be sure your teenager is still in one piece. Our advice is to sit back, take a deep breath, and try to perceive, though it will be difficult, that this feeling you're having is temporary.

Reinvent Your Perception: This Is Temporary

There's a writing about motherhood that went viral this decade on the Internet because it touched a nerve in mothers everywhere. It's by Nicole Johnson (*The Invisible Woman*, Thomas Nelson, 2005). We look at pieces of it as we move through this book, because it so beautifully and perfectly hits on the essence of motherhood and accepting motherhood on so many levels.

EXCERPTED FROM "THE INVISIBLE WOMAN"
BY NICOLE JOHNSON

It started to happen gradually. One day I was walking my son Jake to school. I was holding his hand and we were about to cross the street when the crossing guard said to him, "Who is that with you, young fella?"

"Nobody," he shrugged.

Nobody? The crossing guard and I laughed. My son is only 5, but as we crossed the street I thought, "Oh my goodness, nobody?"

I would walk into a room and no one would notice. I would say something to my family—like "Turn the TV down, please"—and nothing would happen. Nobody would get up, or even make a move for the remote. I would stand there for a minute, and then I would say again, a little louder, "Would someone turn the TV down?" Nothing.

Just the other night my husband and I were out at a party. We'd been there for about three hours and I was ready to leave. I noticed he was talking to a friend from work. So I walked over, and when there was a break in the conversation, I whispered, "I'm ready to go when you are." He just kept right on talking. That's when I started to put all the pieces together. I don't think he can see me. I don't think anyone can see me.

I'm invisible.

INVISIBLE YOU

How many of us haven't felt invisible as a mother? This never-ending whirlwind of runny noses and scraped knees; of incessant demands for food and milk and attention and rides for your children and their friends to every activity imaginable; of more laundry than any human being should ever be expected to do in a lifetime. She was probably up the whole night with this child projectile vomiting, with her as the target. How many diapers had she changed? How many meals had she prepared for this child, painstakingly cutting them into micro-bites so that she wouldn't choke to death? How many hours playing on the floor, cuddling and soothing? How many social outings missed to take care of him when he was sick? And what she has to look forward to—the hours of homework help, of soothing broken hearts, of being talked back to and ridiculed—all done by "nobody."

So now, invisible woman, you have everything you thought you ever wanted, but it's not how you thought you wanted it. You love your family; you love your children. You know they're work, but of course you would do anything for these people, and you're happy to have them—and really could never imagine a life without them in it. You make everything happen and everything work, but somehow, you're invisible. Not the parts of you that your family objectifies to make sure their needs are met, but the intangible part of you that makes you *you*, that makes you not so invisible. But you're not invisible; *you just need to reclaim you*.

Reinvent Your Perception: You Are Not Invisible, You Just Need to Reclaim You

Here's another harsh thing we need to tell you because you need to hear it: much of the reason you feel this way is that your perceptions are out of whack with your reality. No doubt you're probably mourning your "old life" to some extent. Of course you miss your old life, with all its glamour and freedom. But we promise you, your new life can be even better. It isn't going to happen overnight. Entering motherhood comes in stages, too. Changing isn't instantaneous. You can't change by flipping a switch. But you can *start* that way. You can start by changing how you look at things, and as you do, your transition will begin happening.

Jen

My sister-in-law came over, and she looked fabulous. She was so young and thin and dressed up. I felt like a hausfrau standing next to her. I felt like I was never going to be able to look like that again—like the part of me that was *me* was dead. But in time, I saw this was just temporary. I realized I would get that part of me back. It wouldn't be the same way, but I could reinvent it.

It's okay to have a pity party for yourself when you realize nothing will ever be the same again, but make it short. All this stuff that's being expected of you is insane, and it's okay to feel, just for a moment, angry, resentful, deceived, and betrayed, that your fairy tale is not what it promised to be. Feel it, and then get over it. Because the longer you spend dwelling on the past, the longer you're going to have to wait to rediscover yourself in this new light. The key is to stop wallowing in your loss of freedom and your figure, bitching about your husband's dirty socks, and seething over the fact that you can't get anyone to hear or see you. **Because you can be seen and heard, in fact, as soon as you know who *you* are.**

You can't be a mom and not reinvent yourself. You'll end up like Sylvia Plath or Kate Winslet's character in *Revolutionary Road*—and nobody wins there. You have to reinvent if you want to survive. You won't make it otherwise. Real life is hard, and it's not sexy. It's issues about money and who's responsible for what, and when. It's about differences of opinion and space being invaded. It's about feeling crushed and finding a way to expand again.

It's okay to feel crushed and smothered and unhappy *at times*. You're not a bad mom for feeling this way! You've recognized this, and now you can start to find something to make yourself *happier*. Don't beat yourself up about this—it's normal. Changing diapers 24/7 isn't fun. And when the children get older, being a driver and cook and tutor and coach isn't easy, either. But the best gift you can give your kids is to show them a happy mother. **A happy mother loves life—has a passion for life. She has respect for herself and others and a feeling of positivity. She lives life with purpose and laughter and fun and joy.**

In motherhood, about 80 percent is work, and 20 percent is joy. But when you can stand back and look at the big picture, you see that the joy is so sublime, it can make the labor worth it. You just have to be able to step out for a minute—which you can do when you have something for *you*.

MOTHER OF REINVENTION: ELAINE

Doing What You Know Is Right for You— No Matter What You've Been Doing Before

ELAINE BAUER-BROOKS, married, two kids (ages six and four)

BEST ADVICE: *If you dream about things being better, it's probably because you know they should be. But not unless you shake it up.*

"It first dawned on me that I might stop working while I was pregnant with my first child, but I was too consumed by my responsibilities at work to acknowledge it. I was a TV development executive. My job was to create and option new television series, oversee them, manage them, and then do it again! As my due date began creeping closer I started 'nesting' and lost interest in work for the first time in my life. Once Asher was born and I saw that little face, I was never the same again. There was a new 'me' in town, and I knew without a doubt I wanted to be with my baby. But so many things kept me from immediately choosing that path—guilt, habit, and especially fear. A lifetime of reasons converged, and even though I knew what the endgame would be, it just took a while to find the courage and clarity to move forward.

"The most obvious issue was that I made a really good living. I'd be lying if I said that losing that income wasn't a factor. I also grew up with my parents struggling, and I felt it might be irresponsible to 'squander away' my success.

"What confused me most was that though I wasn't really inspired by my career (in fact, I was completely burnt out and pretty darn unhappy), I was dedicated to it. As much as I ached for my baby, my career was a hard habit to break.

"Eventually I decided that even though I loved my job, I was going to have huge regrets if I didn't have the family experience I so wanted. I no longer had to wonder if things would be different at a job I loved. I *had* a job I loved. I spent a full year running my house and hugging my kids. It was the year of super-mom. We didn't run out of toilet paper once! I loved that year.

"Now I've found that I have a little room for something new, so I decided to start something of my own. Thelosangelist.com is a neighborhood guide that allows me to constantly discover new people and places in Los Angeles. I am doing a lot of things for the first time, but I'm inspired and feel it's a genuine extension of where I'm at right now.

"I have an amazing husband. He knew how much I wanted my life to change and how much I loved being a mom. He wanted those things for me so badly that he just said, 'Do it, do it' over and over again, until I finally did. My husband's motto is 'happy wife, happy life,' and though I thought it was just cute when he first said it, I realize it's really profound. My own mother was unhappy and frustrated. She gave up her dreams for her family, and I know that was selfless, but still, I wish she'd have been happy.

"I'm still walking down my own path, uncertain where it will take me, but now I have the family life that I always wanted, and I'm in the building stages of a new project that is very personal and exciting to me. There are still challenges, but I've worked so hard to get to this place, and I won't give up this family time for anything."

Elaine listened to that voice inside her. The one that said, "This isn't working, Elaine. You need to make a change, Elaine." She chose to listen to that over the fear-based voice warning her about what she might be giving up or the mistakes she could be making. Take Elaine's lead. Listen to you. You know yourself best, and that voice within that speaks to you is your truth.

GET TO KNOW WHO YOU ARE *NOW*

It's not easy to separate who you are now from the person you've essentially been your whole life, but it's necessary. When you live in two worlds, you can't comfortably exist in either. *This is not about balance.* You have to be someone new, not who you used to be. When you focus on the person you are now and on the life you live now, you're going to have a lot less chaos and a lot more calm. You're going to feel like you're succeeding rather than failing, because you're going to be in your element again.

Barb

When my children were younger, I really thought I could live in both worlds. I thought taking my preschool-aged daughters to Brazil with friends (who had no kids) was a great idea. Then one of my daughters got lost on a crowded beach, and I had a good dose of reality splashed in my face. It was a turning point for me. What an asshole I was. Who brings three-year-olds to Brazil? Who drags two small kids on a seventeen-hour flight? I was still clinging to my old life. Everything I was doing I was still clinging on to. But once I let that go, I got out of my own way. I was so worried about controlling everything that I was missing the whole experience, and there was something great waiting for me. The experience helped me to realign my perception of things. I let go of my old life and embraced something that was so much better—my family.

How this happens for each of us differs. It doesn't have to be as profound as losing a child in a foreign country. What happens is a mind shift, something that shows you that life has changed, and that it's going to be okay.

Jen

We took Cooper everywhere with us for the first four months: dinners, parties, you name it. He slept in his little car seat, and we were good to go. No problem. One night, however, we went to a small, expensive restaurant with a couple who didn't have kids. We painstakingly carried what now seemed his cumbersome car seat through the tightly placed tables while other patrons stared in horror. The next hour and a half was a blur of visits to the restroom to change vile diapers in an insanely small space (I don't even think they had a changing table, let alone a counter) and walking in and out of the restaurant down a busy street to try to quiet what seemed to be a baby who was being tortured. Not a bite of my overly priced pasta or a sip of the inordinately expensive wine was consumed. I realized I was going to have to find a babysitter. Who could I possibly leave this small, totally dependent baby with? Would I ever go out again?

Reinvent Your Perception:
Your Old Life Is Gone, But Your New Life Awaits

Maybe you used to be a cutthroat executive or an insatiable party girl. Maybe you loved exotic travel and blowing your whole paycheck on a purse and a spa day. Are you the same woman? Probably not to the extent you were. Because of course you can treat yourself to a girls' night out or a new pair of shoes sometimes. But do you really think dragging your two-year-old shopping or to a posh restaurant is in either of your best interests?

MOTHER OF REINVENTION: PAM

Opening Yourself to Change—at Any Phase of Life

PAM BACICH, married forty-five years, mother of two, grandmother of six

BEST ADVICE: *Life is about change, and those who embrace it have the most fun and fulfillment.*

"Motherhood is a journey that lasts for almost three-quarters of most women's lives—but you are actually only at home with your children for about one-quarter of your life. When our children were young, and I was helping to run our family business, I felt I wasn't doing a good job being a mom, a wife, or a boss. When you're in the middle of this part of your life, you think it's going to last forever. It seems that you're buried in a mountain of constant demands from many directions, expectations of yourself and those of others, and the seemingly never-ending responsibilities of being a wife and mother.

"Then one day you wake up and realize that this will soon change. For me it was the day that my son got his driver's license. I sat on the family room floor and cried for an hour. Life as I knew it would never be the same. From that moment on, I would no longer know exactly where my children were. They would no longer *need* me as much. I could no longer be guaranteed that private time when my children were held captive in the car that I had come to treasure.

"The final step came the day both of our children had left home. All of a sudden, my husband and I were on our own. What would we do with all those extra hours we had shared with our children? Would we connect in a new and special way now that we were 'just the two of us?'

"Our business was open late every night, and I could have easily stayed there until 11:00 p.m. every single night. Luckily my husband was wise enough to see what was going on. He started showing up at my office every evening at 6:00 p.m. For weeks he planned something special—a walk by the river, a dinner out, a movie. It was a genius plan and got me to move on.

"Now it was time to spend our extra time doing some of the things we had always dreamed of trying. We purchased a boat and lived on it for four or five months a year, traveling from Southern California to as far south as Zihuatanejo, Mexico, and as far north as Glacier Bay, Alaska. I even learned to drive the boat. I have also been able to indulge in a lifelong passion for photography and have even won awards and had several photography shows of my work, and I'm working on a photography book about the Day of the Dead in Mexico (pambacichphotography.com).

"Do I miss those very special years of being a young mom with young children? Of course I do. More than I would have imagined. But life goes on, and it can be really good and almost magical if you allow yourself to grow and change."

Pam is a wonderful example of someone who put everything into her kids. She gave of herself and wasn't sure what to do with her-

self after they left home. Her ability to find new passions and em-brace life is a prime example of having many chapters in one's life. We are sure her children are inspired by her, just as we are.

DON'T BE A MARTYR

If you think that self-sacrifice for your family is showing them that you love them, stop right there. There is nothing worse you can do for your family, for your marriage, than to be a martyr. Your being fulfilled and interesting as a role model is more important than putting aside what makes you happy and putting everyone else's needs ahead of yours. Your kids are watching everything you do. They don't want a martyr for a mom. You need to show your kids that there is joy for you in adult life. That you have something you are passionate about apart from your family. That there's a spark inside you that's yours alone.

You don't want to show them someone who's worn down by life, who only exists in "survival" mode and not "living" mode. It's good for your kids, your spouse, and you if you take some time to focus on *you*. You owe it to your family and yourself.

Reinvent Your Perception:
Having a Sense of Self Is Not "Selfish"

Some women feel that to be a good mom and wife, complete self-sacrifice is required. That's just wrong. You have to keep something for yourself, and you can't feel guilty about it. The rest of your family are worthy of having something they can call their own, and you are no different. Your children have school and play dates and birthday parties to attend. Maybe they're involved in extracurricular clubs or on sports teams. Maybe your husband sneaks away at the crack of dawn on a Sunday morning to play nine holes of golf or has a regular poker night, or season tickets to see his favorite team. The point is that everyone else who lives in your house has something that's his or hers, outside the house and family. So why not you? It's time to let go of the guilt.

We've been there, and we got out of there. It's impossible for you to open yourself up to figuring out what you want if you're smothering yourself with guilt. If what you crave is an hour away to take a walk or get a mani-pedi, you negate the whole experience if you spend the time wondering what your family members are doing without you, feeling like you should be doing something for them instead. Then you've wasted everyone's time. This seems obvious on the surface, but if you don't have something for *you*, then you won't have anything to give.

Barb

When I got married, I kept my name. I needed a little piece of me to myself. Then I had kids, and I felt like I had nothing of my own. My parents divorced when I was young, and my whole life had been about being independent, but when the kids came along, that changed. I thought I could hold onto my independence, my little piece for me, by continuing to work and making my own money. I had falsely connected dependency with money. I thought I had my bases covered because I worked. But once the kids came along, I realized dependency on my husband went much deeper than money. This wasn't just my husband; this was the father of my kids. So the fiercely independent, "Fuck you if you don't like it" attitude that I'd had my entire life didn't work anymore. I had to let that attitude go. But I still held onto something for myself. Married now more than twelve years, I still haven't changed my name—silly, I know.

When you become a mom, it's easy to feel guilty for taking any time that may seem self-indulgent. Don't do it. You can read a magazine instead of reading another book to your kids. You can watch a show on TV geared toward you instead of *Dora* and *ICarly*. You don't always have to be productive. Let go. Breathe. Take a time-out for you.

Jen

I was really happy giving my all to my family. There was so much joy in every game I played with the kids and every outing we went on. But then not having something for myself caught up with me. I realized one day that I had nothing for myself. I was living with the belief that self-sacrifice is what makes you a good wife and mother. It almost un-did me.

You can love taking care of your family all you want, but not when it comes at the expense of you. The truth of the matter is that self-sacrifice will deplete you, and ultimately you'll have nothing left to give to anyone—especially you. Thinking you have to sacrifice everything for your family will be your demise! You have to have a little piece for yourself. Maybe it's 90 percent for your family and 10 percent for you. Maybe you need a little more; maybe you need a little less. Figure out what percentage you need and work toward getting it. In the next chapter, you're going to fill out a questionnaire to help you figure out just what that percentage is.

Reinventing is about finding a small little piece for yourself, of taking the big picture and shuffling it around a little. Think of your life as a puzzle. The pieces are mostly all there, but you don't quite see the picture they make. Maybe you're not trying to see a picture yet. Maybe you're just trying to get through your day. But if you sit with the pieces one day, arrange them and see how they all fit together, see if any one of the pieces is missing, you could really get a nice picture of how your life is and how it could be with that missing piece in place. You need to take the time to solve the puzzle. Otherwise, instead of a pretty picture you worked hard to piece together, all you have is a forgotten box of pieces haphazardly shoved into the closet. Is that what you want your life to be? A box of random pieces? We'll get into this more as we move through the book.

TAKE TIME FOR YOURSELF!

When you're a mom, no matter how old your kids are, there isn't a lot of time to accomplish all you need to by the end of the day. Your life was packed even before you had kids, and now you have all these other lives to manage, but you still need to carve out time for you. As moms, we're overscheduled and stretched for time taking care of everyone else, but it's time we started taking care of ourselves. But when?

Clinical psychologist Dr. Michelle Golland says what you should be doing is whatever it is that gives you pleasure. It could be a twenty-minute walk around the block; it could be playing the songs *you* want to hear on your iPod. She says, "For me, it's meditating, or just sitting alone listening to quiet music for ten minutes. If I don't take care of me, truthfully I won't be a good partner. If I feel depleted I'm going to feel annoyed at my husband and I am probably going to snap at him. I'm definitely going to be annoyed if he goes golfing, because I didn't take any time of my own."

When you don't take time for yourself, but your partner does for himself, you feel angry, resentful, even used. You wonder why he should be able to have these things while you have nothing. It's because he takes the time—and so should you. What should you do? What do you like to do? Here are some quick ideas:

- Take a college class in something that interests you. It doesn't have to be practical. If nineteenth-century French drama makes you happy, go for it!
- Sign up for an exercise class. Improve the state of your body and mind in one shot!
- Join a book club.
- Take up a hobby.
- Take a bath.
- Have lunch with a friend.
- Read a magazine article.
- Research something that interests you.

Taking twenty minutes a day, even every other day, to really calm yourself, focus on yourself, will not only help you, it will improve your relationships and your family life overall. Remember: happy mom, happy family!

REACH OUT

One of the worst parts of motherhood is the feeling of physical and emotional isolation every mother feels. When you're a new mom, you're sequestered so much with the little one, you barely know there's a world out there. As your little one grows, you tend to do things that will engage and entertain her. You're not really actively seeking out social outlets for yourself—but you should be.

When you reach out to other mothers, you begin to feel you're not all alone in this. Instead of looking at other mothers from a distance, assuming that they're all perfectly content in their new place in life and are running circles around you in the way they have it all together, you'll see the reality. Because if you think even for a minute that you're alone in all of this, you're wrong.

Reinvent Your Perception: You Are Not Alone

Motherhood is the most complicated, challenging, and overwhelming task you're ever going to have to navigate. There's no one manual that tells you how to be a mom. No one has all the answers. No one has it completely together. For every woman you look at and think, "She has it all together," there's another woman or four women looking at you and thinking the same. You're never going to know that until you reach out and share what you're going through with other moms.

Motherhood can be very isolating unless you're around people who are experiencing something similar. When you start spending time with other moms, you see that what they're going through isn't really much different than what you're going through. We're not saying that you have to ditch all your freewheeling single and childless buddies—just bring some moms into your circle. Not only will you feel more comfortable in your own skin, but you may also learn a thing or two about yourself. Instead of fighting the idea of kid-friendly restaurants and playgrounds, you might actually find yourself starting to adapt to them. Instead of having to explain away why you can't do things to people who can't possibly understand, you'll be around people who need no explanation. It's very freeing and comforting.

Another priceless gift is perspective. You'll watch other kids melt down in public, and you'll watch other mothers unravel and fray. You'll watch teenagers talk back to their mothers in public, roll their eyes, or ignore these poor women altogether as they try to reach out to their children. And it won't be schadenfreude you're feeling, but solidarity.

Barb

I had become totally obsessed with being a mom and with all the things you were supposed to be able do. You were supposed to be able to take care of your kids, and I couldn't nurse: fail! I was so exhausted and discombobulated, I didn't feel like having sex ever again: fail! I was so overwhelmed and isolated, I didn't think I was going to make it. My perception of things was completely off, because none of my friends had kids. I had no frame of reference.

One day my husband took the girls to the park so I could shower. When he came home he handed me a woman's phone number. "You need some friends," he said. "Call this woman. I met her at the park. She's really cool." At first I resisted, because of course I already had friends. But then I called her and got a little routine together. We took our kids to the park. I started making schedules for myself of places I could go, and that made me feel more in my element. I had someone to talk to who understood where I was coming from.

The real change came when I went to a Mommy & Me class, where I met Jen. I began to see that all the women were more like me. I started talking and started feeling better. It took me a year and a half of being by myself and living in hell, and all of that could've been avoided if I had just reached out.

DO YOU NEED MOMMY FRIENDS?

You always knew girlfriends were important, but mommy friends are a must! You know all about "BFFs"; we're "MFFs." We met in a Mommy & Me class at Fit for Kids Children's Gym, and we realized almost immediately that the experience was as much for us as it was for our kids. Fit for Kids owner Joan Hushahn explains, "It's about more than your kids having a morning activity or developing socialization skills. You also get to tap into this great network of parents," essentially people who get you and what you're going through. You know what happened with us when we got together this way, and we still have six or seven friends from our class whom we see regularly, with kids our kids still enjoy playing with. Says Joan, "Having a place you can go to and interact with other parents helps you in every developmental stage of your child. You always know you have people you can go to and rely on, and you don't feel so all alone anymore."

You don't need to feel alone. Get out there and meet other moms. They may just become your friends for life.

MOTHER OF REINVENTION:
BETSY (PART 1)

BETSY BROWN BRAUN, sixty-two, married forty years, three kids (triplets, age thirty-three)

BEST ADVICE: *Think about what it is you like to do. What makes you happy, and what you feel you do well. Then explore, ask questions, and listen to people you respect. Start small, with some small commitment that won't make you feel guilty about being away from your primary job . . . mothering.*

"I was a career teacher, nursery school through sixth grade. At the time I got pregnant (with triplets and put on bed rest, because people didn't have triplets back then!), I was teaching kindergarten and loving it. In fact, it might have been my most favorite job I have ever had. *Not* going back to teaching after I gave birth wasn't even in the cards. I loved my job! But when my children were born, I had no help. People didn't have nannies in those days. So that was that. Not only did I fall madly in love with my kids, but my job became raising them. I gave it my all. Having three at once, there was never going to be a 'practice child' for me.

"When my kids were around two years old, I needed more. I needed more cerebral stimulation, and I needed to get out of the house . . . and away from the kids a bit. I didn't feel guilty about this, because I wanted my daughter in particular to have a good model of a mom who wore lots of hats and liked how they all fit. The boys needed that model, too. I don't believe it has to be all or nothing, parenting or career. I do believe, however, that if you are having children, they need to be your priority. I did just enough to be stimulated, but not so much that it affected my children's well-being.

"I knew that any change I made would begin with baby steps, so when I went back to work, it was just a bit at a time. As with all change, bit by bit seems to work the best. People need time to adjust. So I wanted to be sure my kids and I could handle it. And I didn't want to feel overwhelmed. I put my skills as an educational therapist to work and began seeing students on a part-time basis. I hired a UCLA student to help with the kids in the afternoons when I worked.

"As the kids grew and began preschool in the mornings, I wanted more to do. So I put out feelers and became a Mommy & Me teacher at a local school. That position morphed into a few classes, and soon a new career was developing.

"Through a connection, I received a call from a different school looking for someone to run a support group for parents of multiples. That was the beginning of my career as a parenting person. I moved on to become the director of that whole big school, and from there, I was recruited to open an even bigger school.

"My practice as a child development and behavior specialist has snowballed in the ten years since I founded Parenting Pathways®, Inc. I started out running two parenting groups, and within a year those two groups had morphed into ten. Now I run eighteen parenting groups, offer more than twenty single seminars, and have a booming practice in which I offer private consultations to parents of children ages infant through eighteen years old.

"I have reinvented myself several times in my career, from schoolteacher to parent to parenting teacher to school director to creating my own business as a child development and behavior specialist to author. (I am looking forward to adding grandmother to my resume one day soon.)

"I have second-guessed myself at many different career steps of my life. I am often nervous to try something new. But that has never stopped me. I am a *can do* person. I always think I can do it, whatever *it* may be. I might be a bit nervous, but I am always willing to give my best shot. If I fail, I fail, but at least it's not for not trying! I am a problem solver, a solution seeker. I have giant bootstraps that I am forever tugging on (as in "pull yourself up by your bootstraps!"). This comes from my own mother, the most resourceful person I have ever known. She was creative (not artsy), inventive, and imaginative, and she always made lemonade out of lemons. I have lived with that resourcefulness and that attitude my whole life. Thank goodness for that and thanks, Mom.

"Of course I have regrets. Hopefully everyone does, because we learn from our mistakes and missteps, not our successes. Hopefully our lives are filled with enough of both to keep us going.

"Because I believe in the fluid nature of life, I am not sure one ever reaches her full potential. I think we all have different degrees of potential in different areas. Perhaps a better way to think about it is in terms of feeling satisfied. I have felt satisfied by many different things in my life at many different times.

"I am happy to say that I'm not really sure where I am in my career journey. Every single day is different. But I can tell you that I awaken fresh each day and am open to whatever comes my way. Will I write more books? Will I do more media? I really don't know. But I can't wait to find out. I sure hope that I haven't reached my potential yet. I have so much more to do!"

Betsy is an amazing example of "Just do it!" We are sure there have been times when she's wondered whether she will succeed at her next juncture or whether she has taken on something she may not be able to deliver, but she does it. And she does it amazingly, we might add!

THE MOTHER OF YOUR OWN REINVENTION

We said it before, and we'll say it again: You set the tone for your family. If you are relaxed and happy, your family will be relaxed and happy. If you're bitchy, everyone in the house will be affected. Tears will be shed, fights will be picked, doors will be slammed. Don't believe you have all this power in your house? The next time you're in a bad mood, step out of yourself and take a good look at how everyone else is acting around you. So here's a huge reason why reinvention is essential to your family, even apart from you: When you are a more fulfilled person, you will actually be a better mother. If you don't reinvent, you are cheating yourself and your family.

As you work through this book, remember that reinvention is all about the *journey*, not the destination. We all have a final destination; it's six feet under. But until then, we have this wonderful opportunity to grow and evolve and change daily. Unfortunately, we sometimes attach our happiness to a destination: when I get married, when I have kids, when I make a six-figure salary. That's not the way to do it. Finding joy in the process is where you're going to find your ultimate satisfaction.

The need to reinvent happens at different times for different people. It could happen right after you have your first kid, or when your kids head off to college—or any time in between. No matter where you are in the scheme of things, it's important to remember that you are smarter than you've ever been, able to multitask better than ever before, and you have it within you to make this reinvention possible. This is your moment. We reinvented, the scores of women we interviewed for our show and this book reinvented, and now you're going to reinvent, too.

We've interviewed thousands of women over the past five years, and we know having a lack of fulfillment is a common feeling. But we have actually been able to turn things around, in marriages, as moms, and for ourselves.

We can't tell you what the reinvention will look and feel like for you, or if this will be your only reinvention. Other things in life change, so why not you? You may have two, five, seven, or more reinventions, but the lessons you learn here will become the tools that help you through each and every one. We're excited to help you see yourself for who you are now and live your life to the fullest as that person. We both firmly believe that our reinventions didn't help our marriages, they *saved* our marriages, and we go into that in more detail later. Once you alter your perceptions, you need to start managing your expectations, then and now, and this is what we look at in the next chapter. Remember, fulfillment is about living your life as it actually is, not how you always imagined it would be or as it was prior to having a family. It's about expressing your expectations but not imposing them, which is a tough juggling act indeed. We get into that in the next chapter and throughout this book.

NOW YOU KNOW

You're about to embark on a wonderful journey of self-discovery, realization, and fulfillment. We, and the other women you'll meet in this book, have stood where you're standing now, and we've made it to the other side (some of us again and again). Here are the main points of this chapter to keep in mind as you get started:

- It's okay to feel overwhelmed, isolated, invisible, and even alien in your role as mother. We've all been there, but that doesn't mean you have to stay there!
- Motherhood changes you as a person. You need to find the person you are now within the context of your family.
- There is no validation in motherhood *alone*. The only person you can count on for fulfillment is *you*.
- Keep your perspective. You don't have to sacrifice everything for everyone else.
- Reach out. We promise you that other mothers are feeling just like you. Find a "buddy" and talk things through.

Chapter 2

Reinvent Your Expectations

Mapping Out Your Reinvention

I had my first baby when I was thirty-six. I had every intention of going back to work full time once Cooper was three months old, and I followed through. I headed to the office with my breast pump, and the first day was glorious. For the first time since he was born, I felt like an adult again. I went out to lunch, and I pumped while I was on the phone (not that that was fun, but it gave me some freedom). I felt like a productive person in the world. Then came day two. The novelty had already worn off, and I was finding it hard to leave my son. I was starting to realize that this work–life balance I had always imagined would be mine might not work for me.

Shortly thereafter, I got pregnant with my second child; my kids are fourteen months apart (and yes, you can get pregnant while breast-feeding). We weren't planning to have them so close together.

I knew after I became pregnant with Lilah that I would stay home with my kids, but I was confused about it all the same. Actually, I was shocked that I wanted to be home. After my parents divorced, my mom didn't have a career to fall back on, and I always expected I would work because of that. In fact, the thing I was most afraid of was living off my husband financially. And yet I didn't know how to reconcile that with wanting to stay home and raise my children myself.

—Jen

My mom was an A+ mom. She loved being a mother and always looked like she was having a great time. All the kids were always at our house. She was never preoccupied with a career or dinners or parties. There was no planning vacations or decorating a house. We had no money to do any of those things, so we were her entertainment. Life was not serious or planned for my mom—her attitude was always that somehow it would all work out. And strangely, it did.

She is a strong woman, which always made me feel safe as a kid. Nothing was ever a problem, and complaining about things was looked at as ungrateful, as there was always somebody less fortunate than we were. A single mom, she constantly talked to us about sex, drugs, and the ways of the world. She was never a victim, and we were never allowed to be victims. She is a tough act to follow, because she truly dedicated her life to my sister and me and actually seemed content doing it. When I became a mom that was a lot to live up to.

My mother judged me (as all moms do). For her, raising children was her career. She was completely content with her role as a mom and therefore succeeded daily. I, on the other hand, was busy trying to get everything imaginable accomplished and play every role perfectly (mom, wife, career person). My expectations across the board were so high that there was no way I could meet them. I had set myself up for failure.

—Barb

Before you have kids, you have certain expectations. You expect that your life will continue to follow the original plan even after they arrive, simply because you will it to be so. You expect that things might change a bit, sure, but they're not going to change that dramatically. You make yourself believe that you'll soon be able to find a way to cram this small person into your vision of things and continue on with your plan. Then you start to see that you're going to have to start building your life around this little person, not the other way around. We both felt that way at first and went about living the way we expected to at the beginning. We may have done things differently from each other, but we wound up in the same place: We weren't making it. We both felt as if we were failing in some capacity or other. To a point, we were adhering to expectations of the way we had imagined it would be instead of actually living in the lives we were in.

BIGGEST EXCUSE:
I DO NOT HAVE THE TIME TO REINVENT!

You expect you're going to be spending a fair amount of time taking care of your kids, tending to diapers and feedings and dressing, but you imagine that when they get older, you'll have more free time. And then they get older, and in fact you do have some extra time, as they can now feed and dress themselves and go to the bathroom on their own. But that newfound free time quickly gets swallowed by play dates and a list of birthday parties to attend that seems never to end. Later, there's homework and carpooling from social events and after-school activities. Eventually there will be SAT classes and driving lessons and college applications . . . and the list goes on. (And when they grow up and have families of their own, of course Grandma's going to roll up her sleeves and pitch in when she can!) The point is, as soon as you decided to bring this little person into your life, you made a time commitment that you feel like you're never going to be able to meet. And yet you pile things onto your to-do list, a list that's already impossibly long. And you feel terrible when you can't meet all the expectations you impose on yourself.

Time management is going to be key to your reinventing. Trust us: When there's a will, there really is a way. You just need to really will it!

Barb

It was at the end of first grade that I started becoming concerned that India was behind in her reading. The school suggested a tutor forty-five minutes away from our house at $85 per hour, twice a week. I didn't have the time or the money. Jen and I had just signed up our first sponsors. We were working very hard, and I was already spread too thin. I went back to the puzzle of how I could make this happen, how could I move around the pieces to work for me. Where there is a will, there is a way. I ended up driving India on Tuesdays and Fridays, sitting in the car the entire time outside the tutor's house and working. On the days I had to physically be somewhere else, I would ask my husband to take over. All this could have gotten in the way of what Jen and I were doing, but our kids come first. We simply had to find a way to make it work.

NEXT BIG EXCUSE:
I CAN'T REINVENT. I CAN'T AFFORD TO.
I JUST DON'T HAVE THE MONEY.

We say that like anything else, you will never "have the money." So yes, of course, you pay for everything from diapers to college and everything in between, and there never seems to be enough money for any of it. Just when you think you have a little saved to buy yourself a little something special, your car breaks down and poof!—there goes that idea. We get it. Money is a reality, but it doesn't have to stand in the way of your reinvention. Get creative. You have it within you. Learn how to barter or find out what you can do for free. You'll be surprised to find out what's available if you just look. Open your mind and heart, and the possibilities are limitless.

Here's another point about money, which we get into in more detail below: You have more money and time than you realize you do; you just don't spend them on yourself. Think about it. When's the last time you bought something for yourself? A scarf? A pair of shoes? You buy things for your kids all the time—but does your child really need five pairs of shoes? Do your kids really need one more toy? Think about how much all that adds up to and how you could spend some of that money on your reinvention.

One of our favorite frequent guests, relationship expert Dr. Bonnie Eaker Weil, says:

Women need to pay themselves first with both time and money. So when you make your schedule, carve out time for yourself first. When you do your budget, pay yourself first because otherwise there won't ever be anything left for you. Women need to be selfish and take their space. We take care of everything and everyone, and then whatever time is left to spare, we take it. That is why women get sick more often. We need to do it no matter what and do it first before anything else. Whatever does not get done, doesn't get done. Why feel guilty about it? We need to connect to ourselves first. Taking care of ourselves makes us a better mother and lover.

Does your child really need to attend every birthday? Do you really have to spend four afternoons a week shuffling him back and forth to a new activity every day, or is one or two activities enough? Could you instead enlist a family member or hire a babysitter one afternoon a week so you can do something for yourself?

EXCERPTED FROM "THE INVISIBLE WOMAN"

It all began to make sense, the blank stares, the lack of response, the way one of the kids will walk into the room while I'm on the phone and ask to be taken to the store. Inside I'm thinking, 'Can't you see I'm on the phone?' Obviously not. No one can see if I'm on the phone, or cooking, or sweeping the floor, or even standing on my head in the corner, because no one can see me at all. I'm invisible.

Some days I am only a pair of hands, nothing more: 'Can you fix this?' 'Can you tie this?' 'Can you open this?' Some days I'm not a pair of hands; I'm not even a human being. I'm a clock to ask, 'What time is it?' I'm a satellite guide to answer, 'What number is the Disney Channel?' I'm a car to order, 'Right around 5:30, please.' I was certain that these were the hands that once held books and the eyes that studied history and the mind that graduated summa cum laude—but now they had disappeared into the peanut butter, never to be seen again. She's going . . . she's going . . . she's gone!

Ladies, it's time to take a step back. Reevaluate that to-do list and find yourself some time. Be realistic about how much time you have and how much you can accomplish in that time. Remember, time management is going to be key to your reinvention. When Mom fails, Mom is unhappy. When Mom is unhappy, everyone suffers. Why is that necessary? Why do you subject yourself and your family to this? You all deserve better. So it's time to reconcile what's essential and what isn't. What are you expecting from yourself that makes sense in this strange new world of family life, and what doesn't? In this chapter we help you start to see the difference between what's essential and what's not and open a window for you to actually create some time for yourself—believe it or not. Being able to find this time for yourself will actually free up more time in your life, not monopolize it. Don't believe us? Keep reading.

WHAT HAPPENED TO MY LIFE?

In the last chapter, we talked about the fairy tale—the one about the princess who marries the prince and lives happily ever after, with their wonderful children, in the nice, clean house they can easily afford to live in. Part two of that fairy tale is that the princess maintains her identity and her career and her social life and her figure and her wardrobe . . . until the day she realizes that person's gone—to a point at least, she's all but "disappeared into the peanut butter."

Up to the point that your children entered your life, everything had been on your terms: where you went, what you ate, what you wore, how late you stayed out—or even how late you stayed up. Even when you got married, although you checked in with your partner if you were going to be late or to see if he needed you to pick something up or help him out in some way, his demands probably weren't as constant and intense as the demands your children make on you. So why would you think that you can make your life the same as it was before the children came along? Why would you expect you can do everything you used to do, be the same person you used to be? It's a hard place to come to, this realization that there's a wonderful new you where the old one used to be.

Reinvent Your Expectations:
Your Life Has Changed—Embrace It

A critical step in your reinvention is to change your expectations. Time is not infinite. Each day has only twenty-four hours, each week only seven days. Time hasn't expanded since you became a mother. The only thing that has is your task list. Where does this ridiculous set of standards that we daily aspire to meet come from? We would never expect another person to do what we do. Heck, we won't even ask for help! Mothers don't ask for help, because they fear they'll be judged by other moms. It's a sign of weakness, of failure. (She can't handle her kids!) Previous generations used to call on family more to help, but it seems that now we have to depend more on friends or other moms, and it's much harder to reach out.

Who could possibly live up to the standards we set for ourselves? Whether we get it from the celebrity magazines we read or the shows we see on TV—reality TV and otherwise—or just from the way we perceive others, we have a feeling that we just have a lot to live up to. It's somehow not good enough to be a loving, caring mom. We need to be "THE PERFECT MOM." We are also expected to have killer bodies just months after giving birth. Magazines plaster their covers with photos of celebrity moms weeks, even days after having their babies, and exclaim how wonderful it is that So-and-So has "already lost the baby weight!" And we think, as we squeeze into our high-waisted mommy jeans or slide into our sweats or yoga pants, that this is indeed wonderful, and we are somehow less wonderful because our oldest is seven years old and we haven't managed to take off all the weight yet. Is the problem our husbands or the other men in our lives? Are there really men who demand or even wish that their wives could be there for the children and be involved at the school and always have dinner on the table and look great and make a lot of money and always be ready for sex? Are there men walking around telling us that if a woman has not accomplished all of this, she is a failure?

Actually, we put these pressures on ourselves. We don't consciously take them on, however. We get so caught up in the race "to do it all," and things happen so fast, that we go into a survival, reactive mode. And we get trapped there until we decide to take ourselves out of this crazy race—to start becoming active about what goes on in our lives instead of being reactive.

Barb

When we went on vacation, I used to pull everyone's clothes out of the suitcases and neatly put them away in closets and drawers. I would be on top of my family constantly to keep their clothes neatly folded and put away, and I would get upset if things weren't "just so." Lately I've started to wonder why this matters so much to me. Who cares if the clothes are tidy and all in their place? Why was I wasting my time and energy on this instead of enjoying my vacation? The last time we went away as a family, I emptied out the suitcases in a pile on the floor. I told my daughters to take what they needed from the pile and not to worry about putting anything away. All I asked was that they put their dirty clothes in a separate bag. I have to admit, that small decision definitely made this vacation less stressful than the previous ones.

As we said, it's easy to feel as though you've failed when your expectations are unrealistic. Our expectations as mothers are unreasonable, and they don't make sense for our lives and lifestyles. **We need to alter our expectations, not lower our standards.** Whatever expectations you were able to meet before you were a mom, it's okay to let them go. The game has changed; the rules must also change. Would you expect a champion chess player to take command on a pro basketball court? Would you expect a painter to be able to perform surgery?

Reinvent Your Expectations: Let Go of the Guilt

Whoever you were before, motherhood makes you brand new. The worst thing by far that we do to ourselves is to pair these impossible expectations with a terrible sense of guilt when we are unable to meet them and therefore are failing somehow. Then we beat ourselves up more for feeling bad about it and not finding a way to make it all happen. And then we feel bad about that, too, pretty much embarking on a downward spiral of self-destruction, which serves no other purpose than to damage us, and in turn, our marriages and families.

SEE THIS FOR WHAT IT IS

You're not alone, you know. You're not the only woman who wakes up in the morning thinking you're the only one who's "failing" at this—feeling like everyone else has her act together. Nobody else is perfect, and nobody's life is perfect. You may be looking at another mother in your child's pre-K class, wondering how she manages to pull it all together; what you don't realize is that she's looking at you through exactly the same eyes. If you think someone else has this mastered, stop it. Stop it now. Lose that idea, and you'll be amazed at how much better you feel right away.

If every day you wake up and feel that you've failed the day before and are already overwhelmed by what's being asked of you in the day ahead, or, rather, what you expect is being asked of you, change your expectations. Adjust the bar for what needs to be done, and you can scale it without tripping over it all the time.

All the false expectations have to go, so that you can make room to reinvent yourself. You absolutely cannot reinvent yourself if you're too busy comparing yourself to false standards. Reinvention requires all your resources, and it doesn't work if you're wasting your time feeling bad about the things you can't do. You have to focus on what you can do. You barely have time to get even the necessary things done in a day. Why would you waste even one precious minute wallowing over what you can't do?

Celebrate the small miracle of getting your kids off to school without forgetting their lunches and homework and permission slips. And when you do forget, so what? Congratulate yourself for beating the bus to the bus stop. When you watch it fly past you (always much too fast), don't think of it as a personal failure. Pat yourself on the back for finally dealing with the laundry that's been in the dryer since the weekend. When you discover the crusty, near-mildewed batch of laundry behind the dryer that you also forgot about because you were too busy helping your kid finish her kickass science project on Sunday night, be happy that even though she went to bed past her bedtime, he went there clean—and that the laundry can always be cleaned again.

And above all these things, take the minutes you may have wasted beating yourself up and turn them into minutes in which you build yourself up, thinking of the things you can do for yourself, because that's what's going to make you happy, and that's what's going to matter. **What your kids will remember was not that their rooms were organized perfectly, but your state of mind and the mood you shared with them every day.**

CLIMBING OUT OF THE MOMMY RUT

Are you trying to do it all but coming up short? Life coach Erika Feresten explains: "You know you're in a 'Mommy Rut' when that feeling of discontent you're having bubbles over into something else. Maybe your husband mentions that the spaghetti you made for dinner is a little bit overdone—and you take the pot and throw it at him." This and moments like this are overreactions that you have because you're frustrated about what you're not really addressing in yourself. So how do you get out of this Mommy Rut?

Says Erika, "When you realize you're in it, the first step is recognition. One of the things that I did was I took a piece of paper and I wrote down what I felt I was losing and what I was *gaining* as a mother at this point in my life. I was losing regular sleep, but I was gaining this relationship with this little person, my child. Putting it in perspective like that really helped."

Even mothers who've been at it for awhile may need to make some compromises between what they thought they'd be doing and what they actually need to do. Erika says, "If you were a person who once prepared gourmet meals for dinner, and you don't have time to concentrate on making the kind of meal you want to make, let that go for a while and have your husband pick up some prepackaged food for dinner." That's a great solution for during the week, and if you have time on the weekend to whip up a meal that will give you pleasure to make, by all means do it then, when there's no pressure involved.

Being a modern mom is a constant juggling act. There are days when all the balls beautifully stay in the air, and there are others when they all fall to the ground no matter how hard you try. No one can be the perfect parent, wife, and friend all at the same time. If you're feeling overwhelmed, remember that it's temporary. It doesn't feel that way, but it is, and looking at this period from this perspective will help get you through.

A ROOM OF YOUR OWN

Virginia Woolf's extended essay, "A Room of One's Own," published in 1929, was intended as an argument that if a woman wants to write fiction, she needs money and space all her own. She needs something of her own—something that's hers alone. Over the next eighty or so years, that sentiment expanded well out of the realm of an author and has become a metaphor for a woman, and especially any mother, who wants to *live*. Just as we have all these strange ideas that we are terrible mothers unless we fill our days with activities and commitments and notions of things that will make us appear to be better mothers, we also have this strange belief that somehow as a mother, we can't expect to have anything of our own—that our entire existence must revolve around our family's needs.

Reinvent Your Expectations: Take a Slice of the Pie for Yourself and Don't Feel Guilty about It

Jen

I decided to dive into being the perfect mommy and homemaker, and I embraced it. I was in it. I was happy to be in it. I went from owning a business with my maiden name on the door to being Mrs. Pate and Cooper and Lilah's mom, and that was good for me for awhile. But a few years later, I wasn't fulfilled by that anymore. I thought other women had it together. They seemed so sure of themselves. Why not me? What was missing in me? Then I realized that I needed something besides family that made me feel good.

Barb

I grew up with minimal means and a single mom. We lived on government assistance, and it seemed like my mom sacrificed everything for my sister and me. She would give us what she could, but when we asked what she wanted for herself, she always said she didn't need anything—that she was happy giving things to us. So I grew up believing that was what a good mom does—sacrifices everything for the kids. I grew up thinking being a good parent meant giving up everything for the sake of my kids. But I got my wires crossed. Although my mother never wanted for anything in a material sense, she did take what she needed in time. If she needed a break, she took it. She always looked like she loved being a mom, and I made the association that loving being a mom meant sacrificing. Now I realize loving being a mom means feeling fulfilled and giving myself what I need, whether that means time or something else.

There's a misconception about motherhood that wanting something for yourself is somehow selfish. Having something of your own makes you feel worthy. Sorry if that sounds harsh, but as a human, you're worthy and deserving of having something that's just yours. As we said previously, doesn't your partner have something that belongs to him? Certainly your children do. Why not you? You expect to feel fulfilled in motherhood and you aren't—not completely, and that's okay. Reworking that expectation allows you to rid yourself of any feelings of inadequacy. Revising your expectations allows you to connect with other things you're good at. And if you are feeling worthless, how can you feel worthy of having something of your own—even though it's the very thing that's going to help you feel good about your life? This is a vicious cycle of self-destruction, indeed.

MOTHER OF REINVENTION: RISA (PART 1)

"Third Time's" the Charm

RISA GREEN, thirty-eight, married twelve years, two kids (ages eight and six)

BEST ADVICE: *You can't have it all—not at the same time, anyway.*

"I have worked as an attorney and a college counselor, but the most rewarding profession I've had is as a novelist. The transition to full-time writer was really easy in some ways and really hard in others. Easy because suddenly I was home all the time, so I was there for my kids and I was available to run errands and drive carpool and make dinner and do the things that a stay-at-home mom might do. But it was hard because suddenly I was home all the time, and my kids were little and expected me to be with them all the time, and my husband expected me to run errands and drive carpool and do the things that a stay-at-home mom might do, except that I was actually working and I had a deadline and I couldn't do it all.

"So there was a lot of fighting with my husband at first while we figured out a balance. And sometimes we still argue over my work, because I feel like I have to squeeze work time in between morning and afternoon carpool runs, and my kids want me to be their room mom and to volunteer for stuff at school, and it's hard to explain to them that I can't always do those things because I have to write my books.

"After I had kids, I was surprised by the fact that I was okay with lowering my expectations for myself. I'm usually an over-achiever and I'm driven and competitive, and I want to be the best at what I do. But right now, I'm putting that drive and energy into my kids. I don't want to miss out on their childhoods, so I'm willing to keep my career on low right now. I have a million ideas for books I want to write, and I know that I could have a much more successful and lucrative writing career than I currently do if I were to invest all of my time and energy in it. But I'm able to have a somewhat decent career by investing about half of my time and energy, and I'm okay with that right now. I'll have a great career later, when my kids are in college. But if you'd told me fifteen years ago that I'd be saying something like that, I'd have said you must be talking about someone else.

"I do wish, however, that someone had explained to me how hard it is to be big time and to have a life. I grew up during the era of You Can Have It All!, and I really believed it. But the truth is that you can't, and I think that the feminists of the seventies and eighties really misled my generation. The reason you're seeing so many women feeling lost—the reason that this book is so necessary—is because we all bought into that lie. Forget all of that. And be realistic about what you can and can't do. It's not selfish to better yourself, and if you getting a job or taking some classes means that your kid can't play on two different baseball teams, then guess what? He can't play on two different baseball teams. That doesn't make you a bad mom. It makes you a mom with priorities."

Risa so beautifully exemplifies that you need to do what is right for you now. She has gotten out of her own way, and instead of feeling that she's coming up short, she has a wonderful perspective that her kids will be grown and out of the house some day. While she has them there, she may forgo some career success, but that's okay. She knows her priorities, and she's sticking with them.

FIGURING OUT WHAT'S YOURS

Look at yourself prior to having kids: You were a multifaceted person. You had work, hobbies, and a social life. You had friends to hang out with, and you were free to go where you wanted, when you wanted. Somehow when we have kids, a lot of guilt creeps into our lives. We feel guilty if we are not with our kids. We feel guilty if we are ignoring our work. We feel guilty if we take time for ourselves. Look at your husband, if you have one, and think, does he feel guilty for watching sports or playing soccer? Probably not. Somehow, the men in our lives don't carry that kind of guilt. We, too, need to learn that it is okay to let go of the guilt and carve out some time for our needs and desires.

Now it must be becoming clear why we let these false expectations in: It happens when we have a space in our lives, in our
souls, that we need to fill—and we're not filling it correctly. Just
as you try to fill yourself up with a bag of chips or a candy bar
when you need a quick-fix snack, so too are you feeding yourself a
bag of garbage when you shove all these expectations down your
throat. Instead, why not start feeding yourself a steady diet of positive thinking about you? About getting to the heart of what's
yours. Do your kids eat off your plate? Tell them to get their own.
Find your emotional territory and hold onto it.

Barb

I have slept on the same side of the bed forever. When I got married I
explained that to my husband. Well, it just so happens that my side of
the bed has the best view of the television.

For the past seven years that we have lived in our house, my husband has been lying on my side of the bed in his wet robe after he
takes a shower. I have discussed this with him and yelled at him to
"Get your ass to your side of the bed." My side of the bed is my space.
I already have to share everything else with either him or my kids!
Really, is it too much to ask for just this one sliver of space that I can
call my own?

The other night he propositioned me: "If I lose twenty-five pounds,
will you give me your side of the bed?" I had no idea my side of the
bed was such a hot commodity! On the one hand, I do hate the fact
that he has gained so much weight since we got married . . . but on
the other, that side of the bed has been with me for a long time and is
my last "holdout" of independence. I don't think I'll ever give it up!

Forget what's on the surface. Dig deep. Start thinking about
you—not who you think you want to be, not which celebrity

you'd like to aspire to be, but YOU. What will work for you? How can you get to the root of "mine?"

MANAGING EXPECTATIONS AS A WORKING MOM

For mothers who work, outside the home or from home, there's a whole other layer of responsibilities and expectations to manage. "Working moms have to deal with expectation management more than anything else," explains Amy Keroes, founder of mommy tracked.com. "I think that when you come back to work after having your child you have this sense that you'll be able to perfectly compartmentalize your life.

And then reality hits. The days you think you're going to take off and spend time at home with your family are the days that work calls and you can't. The reality of being a mom and having a job is that you're probably not going to your most important meeting because it coincides with your child having a fever and not being able to go into daycare. On top of everything else is the guilt—the guilt that you're not doing a good job as a mother or an employee because you can't give your all to both. Let yourself off the hook as much as you possibly can. It's the only way you're going to survive.

"One thing working moms miss out on is spending time with other moms, at school pickups and drop-offs and at the park after school. When you're working, I think that's more challenging. But hanging around similarly situated people makes you feel normal, so if you can't be involved with other moms in a traditional sense, get involved in an online community like mommytracked.com, where you'll see people on the community section of the site really sharing ideas, commiserating, whatever it is. Finally, look at all you're doing, and treat yourself to something special once in a while, even if it's just taking time to read a trashy magazine or having coffee with girlfriends."

NOT EVERYTHING IS YOUR JOB

You can't be everything to everybody. It just isn't possible. All you're doing by keeping yourself hyper-busy, whether that means overthinking or overdoing, is keeping yourself away from spending time figuring out *you*. Reinvention requires you to set up boundaries and embrace the power of saying no. Saying no doesn't make you a bad person or mean that you're incompetent. It gives you the space you desperately need for your reinvention.

Jen

In retrospect, I wish I could have let go of some of the guilt and spent a little more time on myself in the early years. I made time to work out, something that's very important to me, but other than that, I did everything with my kids. By the time my husband came home from work at night, I was usually frazzled and ready to hand off the kids to him. I think if I had taken a little more time for me, I may have had something left at the end of the day for all of us.

You need to let go of having such unrealistic expectations. Of course there isn't going to be any time left for you if you're busy saying yes to everything. Think about it. Of all the things you do in a day, which ones could you actually *not* do? Make a list and start deciding what not to do. You can't uncover a void in your life if you have no time to reflect and dig deep.

Barb

I have always been a pleaser by nature. My motto has always been "no problem." That was fine before I had kids, but it's not like I learned to say no right away, and I found myself always spinning in circles trying to please everyone all the time. I could have said no to so many things. I didn't know how to say no to anybody back then. That's where I could have gotten some wiggle room.

Reinvent Your Expectations: Embrace the Power of No

Sit back and think about all the things you did today and all the things you could have avoided doing simply by saying NO. Think about how much time you spent on these tasks. Take out paper and a pen and write it out. Add it up. Don't think you have time to do something for yourself? Now you see that you do.

More than that, it's also okay to ask for help when you need it. Ask your mother-in-law or your mother. Hire a sitter or ask a friend for help. Needing help doesn't mean you're an incompetent mom. You'd be surprised how great people feel helping you. And think of it this way: If you ask another mom for help, you're giving her and others an invitation to ask for help, too. Everybody wins.

Your time may be limited now that you're a mom, but you're a better multitasker. Look at all you already do in a day. Your job as a mother requires the essentials: managing people; scheduling; handling finances (which a lot of women do); cooking; time management; organization; planning; and being the nurse, educator, and personal shopper. What other job encompasses so many skill sets and calls for managing them all at the same time? As a mom, you never know what you're dealing with on any given day. Each day throws new curve balls at you, and every day, somehow, you get by. Take the pressure off yourself and don't add other pressure. Remember: You can't get to a better place if you're too busy trying to be perfect and trying to live up to unrealistic expectations.

MOTHER OF REINVENTION: KERRI (PART 1)

Happy Inside, Happy Outside

KERRI HANCOCK WHIPPLE, married eighteen years, three children (ages fifteen, thirteen, eleven)

"Before I became a mom, I was a high school English teacher. I taught for five years before I had kids, and then I quit when my first-born arrived. I did not have to work outside the home for our economic stability, and for that I have been so grateful. I enjoyed being a teacher, but I always knew I would not continue working once I had kids if I was able to stay at home.

"After having kids I was overwhelmed. It was shocking to me, my loss of control. I was at the whim of a tiny infant or a young toddler, and many times that drove me crazy. I was so used to planning and having things go according to plan. But as we know as mothers, plans go out the window a lot, and we have to learn to be flexible and patient and have a sense of humor.

"I used to be aggravated and tense a lot; then I learned to let go. Things went much smoother then—although I learned this lesson far later than I wish I had. I had always been such an achiever. I had always received praise and encouragement for my actions, choices, and accomplishments along the way. This had been what fueled me to keep going and feel confident in where I was headed in my life. When I became a mother, I realized I was on my own. The praise and encouragement that had always driven me was not coming from the little ones I was caring for constantly, and this could be quite depressing. I think this is where my "longing for something more" stemmed from.

"Once you become a mother, the path is wide open. Everyone has different ideas, different techniques, and different ways to approach parenting. The path is no longer as clear as it once was, and this is when I realized it was time to shift my perspective and find something more for me.

"I am now *loving* being a parent. The teenage years make for a frenetic pace of carpools, heavy homework loads, and late-night pickups at social gatherings (I kind of miss the younger years now!), but the foundation we have built over the years has provided us with a very loving and fun family environment that we enjoy a ton. My only regret is that it all seems to have gone by so quickly. Everyone says that . . . but it's true!"

Kerri makes a good point about validation. Do not look for it from your family. Of course those moments when one of your children tells you you're the "best mom ever" make you feel ecstatic, but don't look for that as the only source you have for feeling good about yourself.

REINVENT NOW

Seriously. Start today, right this minute. What have you got to lose?—especially considering how much you have to gain. Reinvent as a woman who enjoys life, who finds pleasure in being a mom, and who is fulfilled. You've realized that you need some sort of fulfillment that you're not getting in motherhood or marriage, so now what? Where do you begin? How do you identify what you need? How do you go about getting it?

This is where the real work begins. There are many questions you need to ask yourself to find the answer. Following is a questionnaire we devised to help us and others get on track to reinvention. Set aside some time when you can really focus on these questions and your answers to them. You can check out our finished questionnaires later in this chapter, when we discuss what specifically sparked us to reinvent.

REINVENTION QUESTIONNAIRE

Fill out the questionnaire below and really give yourself some time to think about the answers. This is the beginning of finding out what you really want and what you have space for in your life. If you're not clear about the answer to a questions, skip it. The answer will come to you. Move on to the next question. And don't overthink! Write down what comes first from your heart and mind. Most of the time, that's where the truth lies.

Today's date: _____

How old are your children? What are their needs now, and how much time do you allocate toward meeting those needs? Do you see those needs changing in the near future? _____

_____

_____

If you have a husband, how much does he contribute to the domestic and parenting responsibilities? Is he able to offer more help if needed?

_____

_____

_____

Are you a two-income family? If so, is that a necessity, and how much money do you need to continue making? If not, are you looking to make money? How much? (Be realistic.) _____

_____

_____

What are you displeased with right now? What do you feel that you're lacking? _____

_____

_____

How many hours per week are you willing to commit to your reinvention?

_____

_____

_____

What are your biggest fears? _____

_____

_____

Now let's talk about desire. This is the time to dream, so let's put it all down in writing. What do you love to do? _____

_____

_____

What are you good at? (If you need help figuring that out, think about what other people always compliment you on.) _____

_____

_____

What are you passionate about? _____

_____

_____

What do you want, and what do you need? _____

_____

_____

What don't you like to do? _____

_____

_____

What is your vision of your "perfect" life? Elaborate. Take your time. _____

_____

_____

_____

Indicate how many hours per week you spend on each of the activities in the chart below. Then indicate how many hours per week you would like to spend on each.

Work

Hours I Devote: _____

Hours I Want to Devote: _____

Kids

Hours I Devote: _____

Hours I Want to Devote: _____

Husband

Hours I Devote: _____

Hours I Want to Devote: _____

Exercise

Hours I Devote: _____

Hours I Want to Devote: _____

Extended family

Hours I Devote: _____

Hours I Want to Devote: _____

Friends

Hours I Devote: _____

Hours I Want to Devote: _____

Downtime

Hours I Devote: _____

Hours I Want to Devote: _____

Hobbies

Hours I Devote: _____

Hours I Want to Devote: _____

Sleep

Hours I Devote: _____

Hours I Want to Devote: _____

Other

Hours I Devote: _____

Hours I Want to Devote: _____

If you worked previously or work now, what did you/do you do? Do you want to continue to use those skills? _____

_____

_____

What are you willing to give up in order to make time in your life for something new? _____

_____

Look at the discrepancies between how you spend your time and how you want to spend your time. How can you change this? Be creative as you figure out solutions. Don't worry if you don't have all the answers yet. Keep reading, and know that each piece of the puzzle will complete the picture as we move on.

GETTING STARTED

If you were stuck on some of the questions, take your time. Don't rush through the questionnaire; it's too important. Walk away and come back to it with fresh eyes and new brain space in a couple of days. This isn't a quick fix; it's a journey. The questions may be difficult, but the answers they draw out of you and the results they'll show are well worth it. Just don't give up.

Reinventing yourself takes time and hard work, and filling out this questionnaire is a big step. Congratulations on committing yourself to working through it and to discovering your new path. How your reinvention will unfold will come through in the way you answered the questions. Look deeply at your answers. Really examine what you've said here. Try to step out of yourself and read through the material objectively. If you didn't know the person who filled out this questionnaire, what would these answers tell you about her?

If you're struggling to get through or understand anything in the questionnaire, get a friend involved, someone you respect and trust. Have that person look at the profile that has emerged and be very honest with you about what it says about you.

Look at your answers and start shuffling things around. With this as your blueprint, it's time to start rebuilding, and to do that you need to find your wiggle room. You may not think there's any wiggle room for you, but there always is—even if it's just fifteen minutes a day. We touched on this when we discussed how important it is to say no.

Now we're going to go deeper. The answers you provided to the questionnaire are like a puzzle. The pieces have to be moved around so you can find your wiggle room. If your questionnaire indicates that you currently only spend two hours a week on exercise and wish you could spend four, what else are you spending your time on that you could change? If you don't know where the wiggle room is, keep looking. If you don't find that time for yourself, you will not be able to reinvent yourself.

Remember, everyone's reinvention looks different and happens on a different schedule. Only you will know what works for you—and if it's working at all. It takes time to figure this all out. We're still figuring it out.

MOTHER OF REINVENTION: CONNIE

The "Accidental" Photographer

CONNIE TAMADDON, forty-one, married, two kids

BEST ADVICE: *Don't feel bad about wanting to make a change. It just means that your brain is functioning. Think of it as a blessing that something inside of you is pushing you to become a better version of yourself.*

"Around the time my first child turned one, I felt a longing to fulfill some creative needs. I looked for a part-time job and accepted a position as an interface designer. I continued working at that job until the birth of my second child, and I was sure I wanted to stay at home with my children. I absolutely loved being a mom. I never had the tied-down feeling that I often hear other moms describe.

"I give my husband credit for turning me on to photography, since I would often complain about his photography equipment being scattered around the house. He told me that I should use it since he was busy working and rarely had time to use it himself as a hobby. When my children were both in school, I had a gallery show of my work at The Photographers Gallery in Palo Alto, and I volunteered regularly, filming and editing fund-raising videos for my children's school's foundation and other nonprofits. I am currently working on a video at my children's high school called *Every 15 Minutes*, which will hopefully encourage the students to not ever drink and drive. My children's book, *Surprising Silhouettes*, which teaches a lesson with questions in the back about the importance of not prejudging others, was published in July 2010, and all of the proceeds from the book are being donated to College Track.

"My children are already in high school, and I am very happy to say that I really don't have any regrets. I knew I could never regret choosing to be able to stay home, without childcare; somehow even back then I knew it would go too fast.

"I am also so thankful that I listened to that little voice that would often annoy me as I lay in bed at night, telling me not to give up on my children's book. Listen to that little voice that bites at the back of your mind and treat it as the gift it is, which just might be your dream if you are brave enough to follow it. Our dreams may change after we become mothers, but hopefully you can keep some part of them alive or find new ones, since your dreams are what will push you to become more than you thought possible."

We love Connie's story because she didn't need to work, but she wanted to find something that was just for her. And when she found it, she expanded it and helped out others with the outlet she found. Picking something you love to do, tapping into your passion, and then turning it into something positive in the world: It's a wonderful story about how helping yourself really does help others!

JEN AND BARB:
OUR REINVENTIONS

In the last chapter we touched on what made each of us want to reinvent. We had come from totally different places, raised in completely different ways. The only thing we shared was that we were children of divorce, and even though our marriages were different, we both knew that we definitely wanted to stay married and be there for our kids. In Barb's case, reinvention had a lot to do with reconciling her perceptions of what was supposed to be with what actually *was*. Both of us wanted more. It wasn't that we were unhappy and wanted something different. We just felt something was missing. We didn't need to replace what we had; we needed to enhance it—though for different reasons.

You Can't Be Everything:
Barb's Reinvention

Barb

I felt like I wasn't doing anything as well as I used to. I felt the expectations were so high of what I was supposed to be. My house was supposed to be perfect—with fresh flowers. I was thirty-five and supposed to look twenty-five. My kids were supposed to be perfectly dressed and perfectly clean all the time. I put myself under too much pressure.

For Barb, reinvention came when she was frustrated about being pulled in so many different directions and not being able to do anything—motherhood, her career—as well as she expected to. When she was able to see this more clearly, she made a choice to let up and let go, which opened her up to new possibilities.

QUESTIONNAIRE: BARB

Let's start with the facts.

Today's date: *August 2004*

How old are your children? What are their needs now, and how much time do you allocate toward meeting those needs? Do you see those needs changing in the near future? *My twin daughters are two years old, and they require my attention 24/7. When they start preschool next year, I'll have between 9:00 and 2:00 without hearing "Mommy!"*

If you have a husband, how much does he contribute to the domestic and parenting responsibilities? Is he able to offer more help if needed? *We're probably 70/30: I, 70 and he, 30. Yes, he could give up his TV time and step up his game to give me the opportunity to even take a shower. He's literally eating chips and salsa and watching TV while I make beds. I think he also may be unfulfilled.*

Are you a two-income family? If so, is that a necessity, and how much money do you need to continue making? If not, are you looking to make money? How much? (Be realistic.) *Yes, we are a two-income family, and before that we were a two-income couple. I've always worked since I was sixteen and have been able to support myself on my own. Yes, it's a necessity for me to keep working in order to keep the lifestyle we're living right now. We could downsize some things, but I'm not sure if that's what we want.*

What are you displeased with right now? What do you feel that you're lacking? *I'm not inspired by my job. I don't feel my husband is pulling his weight. I feel like I'm failing and I'm isolated. I feel like I don't do anything right. I feel like a voyeur in my own life, like my life is happening and I'm going through the motions, but I'm not actually there. I feel beat up. I've* *lost the pep in my step. I feel downtrodden and overwhelmed and exhausted. My life is so monotonous. It's the same thing over and over with my marriage and with my kids: bottles, breast pump, dirty diapers, the park, in the stroller, out of the stroller. I don't feel there's any end in sight.*

How many hours per week are you willing to commit to your reinvention? *Twenty hours per week. I want to be able to drop my kids off at preschool and pick them up and attend play dates, and they'll soon go to school five hours a day. That would still leave me with an extra five hours to do a couple of personal things and manage my house.*

What are your biggest fears? *Not being good enough. My marriage failing. Not enjoying being a mom.*

Now let's talk about desire. This is the time to dream, so let's put it all down in writing. What do you love to do? *Talk to my friends. I love to hear people's stories. It's my favorite thing. If I had the choice between playing tennis and hearing three women's stories, I would always take the latter. I'm intrigued by people's journeys in life and what makes people do what they do. They inspire me.*

What are you good at? (If you need help figuring that out, think about what other people always compliment you on.) *I'm a great listener. My husband always compliments me on how I can go to a party and get any piece of information out of anybody. Maybe I should have been a CIA agent.*

What are you passionate about? *My passions have changed over time, but right now I'm passionate about my kids. I'm trying to figure out this whole mommy world. It's become an obsession of mine. I know how I'm handling being a mom right now isn't the "right" way for me. I don't think everything about it is working, and I feel like there has to be a better and more fulfilling way to be a mother. I also love to travel.*

What do you want, and what do you need? *I need validation through my work, my husband, and my children. I need to feel that I'm doing a good job. My children are too young to offer me that, so I feel like I don't have a lot of self-worth. My husband is having his own set of adjustments, so I feel invisible.*

What don't you like to do? *Cook. I hate it.*

What is your vision of your "perfect" life? Elaborate. Take your time. *To be able to do drop-off and pickup with my kids. To be financially self-sufficient. To enjoy my family instead of constantly being exhausted and depleted. To get some breathing room. To have a few seconds of every day that aren't accounted for.*

Indicate how many hours per week you spend on each of the activities in the chart below. Then indicate how many hours per week you would like to spend on each.

Work

Hours I Devote: 40
Hours I Want to Devote: 20

Kids

Hours I Devote: 24/7 (except for when I pee)
Hours I Want to Devote: 50

Husband

Hours I Devote: 2 (if even that)
Hours I Want to Devote: I don't care how many hours we spend together—I just want to have fun with him again. Everything feels like work right now.

Exercise

Hours I Devote: 0

Hours I Want to Devote: 0 *(You couldn't pay me to exercise. I'd rather starve.)*

Extended family

Hours I Devote: 40 *(my mom and my mother-in-law are taking turns living with me. It's great for my kids, awful for my marriage.)*

Hours I Want to Devote: 10 *(with a very clear rule that an invitation will be required before popping by)*

Friends

Hours I Devote: 0

Hours I Want to Devote: 10

Downtime

Hours I Devote: 0 *(unless you count getting the grey out of my hair)*

Hours I Want to Devote: 5

Hobbies

Hours I Devote: 0

Hours I Want to Devote: 0 *(Talking to my friends is my hobby.)*

Sleep

Hours I Devote: 35 *(5 hours a night, but it's interrupted)*

Hours I Want to Devote: 49 *(interruption-free)*

Other

Hours I Devote:

Hours I Want to Devote:

If you worked previously or work now, what did you/do you do? Do you want to continue to use those skills? *I work in sales and marketing. Yes, I* *think no matter what I do, I'm going to have to sell it, so my skill set will come in handy.*

What are you willing to give up in order to make time in your life for something new? *What changes can I realistically make? I don't feel like there's anything I can give up. I guess I need to rearrange or reconfigure my situation. It's not like I have any downtime right now. I can't give up working because I enjoy it, my time with hubby is at a bare minimum, and the only place I can pull from is my time with my kids, but I'm such a control freak that I can't really imagine doing that.*

Barb's Story

I decided to keep working after my twins were born. I got up every morning at 6:00 a.m. and worked from 6 to 9. Then my husband would leave for work, and I took care of the kids. I really stuck to a schedule. I thought I had it all under control. Then things just started going wrong.

Working a few hours in the morning was proving not to be enough for the job, and I started having to go in to the office a couple of times a week, which meant another commitment for which I had no time. Soon, not having any time for myself started taking its toll. I came out of the gate strong. I thought I could handle all this, and I thought other women were wimpy. Before I had kids, I would see a mom in the grocery store with her kid lying on the floor having a fit, and I would think, "She doesn't know what she's doing. That will never be me!" I ran a company; how hard could being a mom be?

Then it all started unraveling—wanting to be supermom, wanting to be a superstar at work, wanting to prove to my own mom how good I was at all of it. I craved validation across the board and couldn't find it in anything I was doing. With the sleep deprivation compounding things, everything, or so it seemed to me, started falling apart. I couldn't keep on top of things at work; at home, one of my daughters fell out of the bed, and I felt like my relationship with my husband had become strained. Our lack of intimacy wasn't helping any. The guilt over all of it was incredible.

On top of it all, I felt very isolated and alone. None of the friends I had were mothers. And now, very unlike the woman I had been before becoming a mother, I felt like I had deteriorated into the crazy woman in the supermarket who couldn't control her kids—and I felt everyone else was actually better at it than I was.

I had nobody to talk to about it—or at least I didn't believe I did. I didn't realize everybody was feeling the same thing until I really started talking to other moms. I kind of put myself out there, and I saw that other moms were feeling just like me. Once I changed my expectation, once I realized that the house didn't have to be perfectly clean, it took the pressure off and I felt better. When I put myself out there, I learned that other women were not having as much sex with their husbands, were frustrated about not having any "me" time—and also had experienced having their children falling out of the bed!

When "All" Isn't Enough: Jen's Reinvention

Jen

I didn't want my kid to be home with a nanny all day. I wasn't comfortable with that. I think it has to do with having had my children a little bit older, of seeing other friends have kids and experiencing how fast the time goes. I knew I wanted to be there, home with my kids, especially before they started school. I was aware of the temporary nature of that baby time, that before I knew it they would be in school and I would regret having not spent time with them. I enjoyed it and embraced it. I even thought that this would make the perfect family. I thought, "This is so perfect. My husband loves it, the kids are loving it, I'm happy." Then I realized that it wasn't working.

In Jen's case, reinvention was sparked by something other than craving "more"—a filling of a void. In Jen's mind, it seemed that everything was as it should be. She was able to stay home with her kids, but there was a frustration festering, on both her end and her husband's, over financial issues and domestic responsibilities, and it had the potential of blowing up.

QUESTIONNAIRE: JEN

Let's start with the facts:

Today's date: *May 2007*

How old are your children? What are their needs now, and how much time do you allocate toward meeting those needs? Do you see those needs changing in the near future? *Cooper is 3½ and Lilah is 2½. Lilah needs me 24/7. Cooper is going three days a week for half a day to nursery school. In the next couple of years, they're going to both be in school—maybe not full days, but it will be a big change for me.*

If you have a husband, how much does he contribute to the domestic and parenting responsibilities? Is he able to offer more help if needed? *He contributes very little to domestic responsibilities. Although he's a loving dad and does contribute to the parenting responsibilities when he's around, the majority of the responsibility falls in my lap. He's working a lot, and he just doesn't have much time. But his job is one that changes, so he may have more time in the near future.*

Are you a two-income family? If so, is that a necessity, and how much money do you need to continue making? If not, are you looking to make money? How much? (Be realistic.) *We were when we got married, but I gave up my job as a casting director when Cooper was five months old and I found out I was pregnant with my second child.*

What are you displeased with right now? *Although I enjoy being with the kids, I'm feeling tired of being a housewife. I want more stimulation. I feel that my husband doesn't understand what I'm going through. He thinks my life is so easy. I'm getting frustrated.*

What do you feel that you're lacking? *Self-worth and purpose outside of my family. Financial independence. Intellectual stimulation.*

How many hours per week are you willing to commit to your reinvention? *I don't know how to find the time right now. I'm not sure where it can come from, but I know I need it.*

What are your biggest fears? *That I won't feel like a worthwhile and complete person when my kids get older, that I will be forever financially dependent on someone. That I won't have something that's just mine.*

Now let's talk about desire. This is the time to dream, so let's put it all down in writing. What do you love to do? *I love to do yoga, I love to read, I love to hang out with my friends, I love to laugh, I love to talk to people, I love the arts, I love nature.*

What are you good at? (If you need help figuring that out, think about what other people always compliment you on.) *I am good at helping people get through problems. I have an even disposition (most of the time!) and a positive outlook on life. I'm athletic, and I have a lot of energy. The biggest thing for me is that I'm a "glass half-full" person.*

What are you passionate about? *My family. And I mean that for my husband, my children, my siblings, my parents. I'm passionate about appreciating life and getting everything out of it.*

What do you want, and what do you need? *I want my husband to appreciate what I'm doing—that my work is as important as his and that it's appreciated. I want something to look forward to other than my family. I need more understanding from my husband that though I am lucky to be home with our kids, it's not easy.*

What don't you like to do? *I don't like to clean the bathrooms or mop the floors.*

What is your vision of your "perfect" life? Elaborate. Take your time. *Living around family and friends with enough money to not be stressed out, with having time for myself. I want to feel like I have some independence and that I'm understood. I want to be stimulated emotionally, physically, and intellectually. Mostly I'm missing the intellectual stimulation now.*

Indicate how many hours per week you spend on each of the activities in the chart below. Then indicate how many hours per week you would like to spend on each.

Work

> *Hours I Devote: 0*
>
> *Hours I Want to Devote: 0 (Interesting that I ended up with a job, but that was not what I wanted when my reinvention began. I had no idea it would come in the form of a job.)*

Kids

> *Hours I Devote: 24/7 (all my time except for exercise and an occasional date night)*
>
> *Hours I Want to Devote: Maybe 21/7! not much less. I'm not looking to escape them. I just need a little something added to my life.*

Husband

Hours I Devote: 20 (awake hours and this is not alone time) He's working all the time right now so I see him first thing in the morning and he tries to get home for dinner, which doesn't always happen. Usually an hour before bed and on the weekends.

Hours I Want to Devote: 32, but I would settle for 4 alone hours. I wish his work hours were not so long and I wish he was home for an early dinner every night.

Exercise

Hours I Devote: 5
Hours I Want to Devote: 7–10

Extended family

Hours I Devote: 0 (We were on location for my husband's work in Wilmington, North Carolina, and my family is in Los Angeles and Chicago.)
Hours I Want to Devote: 20 (I wish I could see a member of my family every day.)

Friends

Hours I Devote: 6 (this is with kids however) I've made a couple friends—one of them is my lifeline. I picked her up at a park. Thank God for her. I talk on the phone a lot to my friends though not nearly as much as I would like. I miss my old dear friends in LA. I'm a girl's girl so that's hard for me not to be close to them. I'm very loyal to friends and I miss spending time with people who really know me.
Hours I Want to Devote: 6 (but without the kids)

Downtime

Hours I Devote: 0. What downtime?
Hours I Want to Devote: 7 (I'd love even an hour a day to just sit and read a book or watch TV.)

Hobbies

Hours I Devote: working out (see above) 5

Hours I Want to Devote: 7–10

Other

Hours I Devote:

Hours I Want to Devote:

What are you willing to give up in order to make time in your life for something new? *What changes can I realistically make? I can get more help for the kids so I have two afternoons a week to myself. But I feel guilty spending money and feel like it's my job as a stay-at-home mom to be with them every second. (In hindsight, I'm not sure why I felt like I needed to be a martyr. My kids would have been just fine if there were a few more hours a week that I wasn't with them.)*

Jen's Story

My husband, a writer and director, traveled a lot, and before the kids were in school, the whole family would go with him on his trips. When a project landed him in North Carolina, we relocated for awhile, even selling our home in Los Angeles. My husband was happy in North Carolina and wanted to stay; I was starting to feel a little brain dead, a little incomplete, and craved intellectual stimulation. On top of that was the money thing. My husband, who was bearing the financial burden of the family, started saying things like, "If you could just make 100k a year and still be around for the kids, that would be so helpful." I remember being so angry. If that job existed, women would be lining up at the door!

But beyond making me angry, it also gave me the push I needed. I was never comfortable living off his salary, and this really brought that home. He fired me up and gave me clarity. I had no idea what I was going to do, but I knew I was going to do something. I knew that if the financial pressure was a problem, I needed to take it off the table. My family came first, and I wasn't clear how I was going to make it happen—only that I *was* going to make it happen. I had this feeling that there was a voice inside me that needed to be heard and that I had to move back to LA.

The struggle caused a lot of stress on my marriage, especially as I didn't know exactly what I was going back to LA for. I just knew I wasn't finished with LA yet. I needed to have a reason to get up in the morning other than my family. I also needed to contribute financially. The financial stress was going to be even greater in LA.

I finally hooked up with Barb and connected with her on something that made sense for both of us. Four years later there have been plenty of growing pains, and it's taken awhile to shift the responsibilities in my home, but now that I have my sea legs, I'm happier. My husband has less financial stress, and he seems to be so proud of me and admire what I'm doing. We have more to talk about other than our kids—and my kids are thriving. I'm still there to put dinner on the table and pick them up after school. I don't mean that it hasn't been a bumpy road, but it's feeling really good right now.

MOTHER OF REINVENTION:
BECKY (PART 1)

From the Newsroom to the Nursery

BECKY BEAUPRE GILLESPIE, thirty-eight, married, two kids (ages nine and six)

Author of *Good Enough Is the New Perfect*

BEST ADVICE: *Don't try to be perfect, and don't be afraid to make mistakes. Sometimes pursuing what you really want is scary, but that doesn't mean you shouldn't do it.*

"When I was pregnant with the older of my two daughters, I thought I had everything: a perfect job, a perfect new family. I was so happy. I had this long maternity leave planned—and then I'd head back to work and bury myself in a satisfying new project. It seemed like everything was falling into place. Except it didn't work out that way at all. I loved being home with my daughter, and it was hard to envision returning to the paper and working the same hours—and as obsessively—as I had before she was born. Suddenly I had a new love in my life, and everything had been turned upside down. Was I going to have to choose? Could I have both?

"When it was time to go back, I thought the most obvious way to 'have both' was to work part time. *Wrong.* I was miserable. Cutting back my hours meant giving up all the parts of my job that I loved the most. Without them, it was hard to justify being away from Beth. I hadn't expected to miss her so much. Or to feel so awful when I missed something new. I was filling in for an assistant city editor the day Beth took her first steps. That crushed me.

"I left work most days feeling like I'd failed to accomplish much of anything. To make things worse, my husband was an attorney at a major law firm; his hours were brutal. But I thought I had to 'stick it out.' I hadn't been raised to be a quitter. I didn't want to give up a lifelong dream; I thought that would be the same as failing. But failing in whose eyes?

"I think this is a big challenge for our generation: When we're so focused on being 'perfect' and living up to other people's expectations (perceived and real), we struggle to make the decisions that are right for our lives. We stick it out in situations that make us miserable or don't fit our lives because we're afraid that giving up means failing.

"I eventually realized that it was ridiculous to 'stick it out' in something that made me unhappy just because it fit my old plan or was something I thought other people expected of me. So I reinvented myself from newspaper reporter to stay-at-home mom, but I still needed more reinvention. Reinventions are works in progress. We have to keep making adjustments as life changes.

"One summer I started a small networking marketing business, simply because it was outside my comfort zone. When my friend Hollee e-mailed me asking if I wanted to write a book about working motherhood with her, I ignored my initial impulse to say I didn't have time and told her I'd love to do it. The business wasn't a good fit, although it helped get my mind working in new ways. The book was exactly what I wanted to do, and I was ready to dive in when that opportunity presented itself.

"I was excited, and although I didn't know exactly how things would unfold, I knew exactly what we needed to do to get started. It was a writing project—the thing I most loved doing—but on a much bigger scale. As we got started, I had a revelation: Reinventing my life wasn't about how I allocated the hours—it was about focusing on things that I loved doing. Things I was good at, things that made me feel proud. It's funny how we find all the hours we need when we really love what we're doing.

"Hollee and I didn't just want to write a book; we wanted to make a difference. We wanted to advance the conversation about working motherhood and work–life balance by contributing new ideas, and we wanted to transform our own lives in the process. We also developed a great system of covering for each other when one of us had an illness or a crisis or needed to do something with our kids. She's the one who taught me how important it is to ask for help. I also learned how imperative it is to support each other emotionally.

"Our daughters struggled at first with all the upheaval. I worked a lot to make the deadline for our manuscript. They went to after-care at school more often—and I sometimes had to spend entire Sundays in my home office, writing. Occasionally they'd say, 'I hate your book! You love it more than you love me!' (They'd later admit they didn't really believe this.) But my husband stepped up in a way that has forever changed our family. He took over cooking and grocery shopping; on the weekends, he took them to their activities. His level of involvement has made us equals—and I think it's the best gift we ever could have given our children.

"I wish I'd let go of that feeling that I had to be everything to everyone much sooner. Feeling that I had to be the perfect mom (and do everything myself) and still somehow have the perfect career made it impossible to see how many options existed. All I saw was a narrow path that was very difficult to maneuver. Once I opened my mind up and accepted that it was okay to make mistakes, that I didn't need to feel guilty, all I saw were opportunities. They were everywhere. All I had to do was choose the path that felt best and start running."

Becky brings up an important point to keep in mind. There is no such thing as "perfect." You are not "settling" if you are not achieving some preconceived goal from somewhere that you aren't doing everything expected of you. You, like Becky, are just doing your best!

DO IT FOR YOU, DO IT FOR THEM

There's a serious side to all of this, which we had to learn the hard way: If you don't do something, eventually you are going to implode, and when you do, it will not only hurt you, it will affect everyone connected to you. If you don't make a change, you'll be an unhappy mom, your marriage will suffer, you may have health issues, and you'll be a terrible role model. Sorry, but that's just the way it is.

Reinvent Your Expectations: Adapt or Implode

Barb

Prior to my reinvention I had constant spurts of frustration, of feeling like a failure playing out daily, and I would go into the bathroom (the only place I could hide) and cry. I remember one time when the babies were infants and I had to go into the office for a few hours. I came home a little while later even though I had so much work to do and put my daughter India in the middle of my bed, surrounded by pillows, for her nap. I went to the backyard to talk to my mom, then I heard a loud thump. I ran to my bedroom, and there was India on the hardwood floor, crying. She had scooted herself backward off my bed—a skill she had apparently just developed. I was hysterical. I felt like such an unfit mother, that anyone could take care of these babies better than I could.

Before you implode, make a change. It can be minor: Just don't wait until you have a full-blown meltdown. If you feel that you may have already imploded, don't worry—it's not too late for you. We've been there, and we came back. But if you haven't gotten there yet, learn from our mistakes. It's taken us years of trial and error and unfortunately involved a lot of stress and heartache to get to where we are now. But you don't have to repeat our mistakes. Our goal is to help other women get there without as much struggle as we've been through. This doesn't mean that you won't have any struggle at all, but if we can help alleviate some of the stress and heartache we went through, then it's all worthwhile!

MOTHER OF REINVENTION: LISA

A Blog Is Born

LISA BORGNES GIRAMONTI, married, one child

BEST ADVICE: *Don't worry if Act One doesn't pan out. You can always create an Act Two (or even Act Three). Remember that the little things turn out to be the big things, and that true fulfillment comes when you are in balance with yourself, your family, and the world.*

"I was a copywriter working in New York and Los Angeles for ad agencies like Saatchi and Saatchi, Ogilvy and Mather, McCann-Erickson, and NW Ayer. After my son was born, I knew I wanted to be around to see him grow up, and that a crazy, high-powered job like advertising wouldn't work for me anymore. I struggled for awhile. I wrote a couple of screenplays, I did a few freelance jobs, but I wasn't happy.

"I decided to stay home and raise my son full time, but there was still a creative spirit inside me trying to get out. By this time I had become entranced by the world of blogs, and design and style blogs especially. All these fascinating people who had a specific point of view and wanted to share their passion with the world. I was entranced by the creative freedom and global reach that blogs provided. My itch to start writing again had been growing for a while, and I felt an overpowering urge to start a dialogue with all the like-minded souls in the world.

"I started my blog one night in October 2008 and wrote my first entry. For two months, I wrote and wrote. I had a viewership of three (me, my mom, and my husband). Then in January 2008 I sent an e-mail to five of the top style bloggers I most admired, telling them what an inspiration they had been to me and that I had just started a blog of my own. I also sent them photos of my home, which I had just redecorated. Two days later, Heather Clawson of the famed blog Habitually Chic did a huge post about my house, and in one day, my readership jumped from three to 2,700! Now, three years later, I've garnered over 500,000 unique views and have readers in over 140 countries.

"My husband was thrilled that I wasn't grumpy anymore! He loved that I could be creatively fulfilled while still being around to take care of our son. My husband is a fabulous equal partner. As I'm typing this, he's downstairs making me coffee and our son breakfast. His wish is simple: He just wants me to be happy (or as he says, "Happy wife, happy life.") He is an avid cyclist, so we make sure to coordinate the weekends so that each of us has a bit of sacred alone time. That's very important for us as a couple. Everyone benefits.

"The blog has been amazing. So many opportunities have arisen from it. I recently had a solo art show at the ACME Gallery in Beverly Hills for my postmodern embroidered samplers. I have been an online columnist for *W Magazine*. I have been invited to give a lecture on hearth and home on the East Coast. I've just started filming a series of short webisodes for my blog called 'The Domestic Explorer.' which I'm very excited about. And of course, the media attention has been very flattering. There is an upcoming home decor book called *Undecorate*, featuring fifteen homes in America not designed by designers, and mine is in it.

"In retrospect, I wish someone had told me not to worry so much—that things would happen in the order they're meant to happen, and to never lose sight of what I loved doing, because it was my passions that would eventually steer me to the right place."

Once again we hear it: passion, passion, passion! Lisa is proof once again that having a passion keeps you and everyone around you happy!

IT DOESN'T HAPPEN OVERNIGHT

At forty, we decided that we wanted to do something through which we could be fulfilled as women, financially contribute to our families, and still be with our kids. Of course your reinvention will look different. It could be that you're a stay-at-home mom looking for a little time for yourself, perhaps just an hour a day or week to do something just for you. You could be a working mom looking to spend more time with your kids. Or maybe your old job isn't working for you, and you're looking for a new career. Maybe you're perfectly happy doing what you're doing, but you just want to find the time to take a few classes. **Remember, it's not about the BUT, it's about the AND. What can you do to enhance the life you love?**

There's a gestation process at work here—and there's going to be a lot of trial and error as you hone in on your reinvention. If one idea doesn't work, try on another. Just don't give up the process. Right now is the time for you to explore your passions, strengths, and needs.

This is the time to do something you love, something you would do for free, something that won't feel like work. Something you feel really passionate about. You have to be willing to roll up your sleeves and get dirty. You have to be ready to find worth in yourself on a deeper level. Open your mind. You will find more self-confidence as you go through this journey. The more confident you are in yourself, the easier everything else will be. But the only way to build your confidence is to keep putting yourself out there in terms of your reinvention. Keep practicing YOU.

Jen

I spent about six months exploring another business opportunity before Barb and I began our journey with our show. I had an idea for a one-stop shop for moms. Imagine one building that had everything: a post office, a nail salon, a kid's drop-off, exercise classes, a car wash, dry cleaning, a coffee shop, a cafe—you name it! It was going to be called "The Daily." I had the creative idea, and I was working with a friend who was wonderful at business. I was getting great companies to say that they would be a part of our venture, I was looking at real estate. However, my business partner, even though she loved the idea, didn't see how the numbers were going to work. She was living in another state and would have to quit her high-paying, high-powered job. We ended up putting the idea on the back burner. I am so happy that Barb and I came up with the idea for our show, but I wish The Daily existed for me now!

Even though it didn't work out, I learned so much from the time I spent on trying to start up that business, and I don't regret one minute of it. It started my search for something new in my life, gave me a reason to get up in the morning and be excited about something. It set the tone for my reinvention and my fulfillment.

Reinvent Your Expectations:
You're Probably Not Going to Nail It the First Time

You'll find your own speed and comfort level. Even we have different approaches. Jen likes to dive right in without wondering how deep the water is; Barb is more calculated in her approach. And yet we both come to the same place. Whatever it is that you want to do, don't expect miracles or instant fixes. One thing it takes to reinvent is courage; another is time, and the perspective that time gives you. It's okay to be a little wary of what's on the other side of your reinvention. That's a good thing. It slows you down just a little bit so you can take it in as it's all happening and work it out as you go along. Remember, change is good!

Whether you want a new career or a new body (sorry ladies, the old one is gone), it may take a few tries to realize your vision. Even though on paper it looks like starting your own cupcake business is the way to go, you may find that you don't have the capital right now to make it happen or that the workload is so big that it will interfere with your family. Remember, this is your time to really do what you want to do—take your time to do it right!

There is no wrong or right decision, but your inability to make a decision will prevent you from carrying out your own reinvention. What is the worst that will happen? It won't work? So what? You will learn something from each experience and will ultimately be on the right path for you.

MOTHER OF REINVENTION: KABREL

Refresh, Renew

KABREL GELLER-POLAK, forty-seven, married fifteen years, two kids (ages eight and four)

BEST ADVICE: *Be flexible, creative, adaptive, constantly curious, and self-accepting. Isn't that the same as reinvention?*

"I did not make this most recent change in my life because I was feeling empty, something was missing, or I 'just needed more.' I was not in a conversation with myself about how I was going to find a way to 'reinvent' myself, nor had I felt the way many of my other mom friends had: 'I'm feeling bored, I wish I had something more to do'; 'I wish I had a job that would allow me to work when I want and also be with the kids'; 'I used to have the greatest wardrobe before I had kids, now I wear the same thing every day.'

"It never occurred to me that I needed reinvention. What happened to me was more of a 'refresh,' like what happens on your computer. All the past and present data are in front of you, everything you have deliberately input and all of the responses to that information, but when you hit that button everything that awaits you appears. I believe my personal shift grew out of new realizations about who I am and who I want to become.

"Prior to having kids I had a successful, gratifying career. I owned my own company and employed eight people as an agent in the movie industry. I traveled, attended movie premiers, had a black belt in shopping, went to spontaneous girls' nights, represented Oscar winners, and made great money. And for the most part, I did what I wanted with that money.

"When we decided to have children, I came up with a great plan: I would take three months off, then I would build out a nursery in my office, hire a nanny, and bring them both to work with me! But by the time my daughter was about six months old, going to the office to talk about *Home Alone 12* or the latest Snickers commercial could not hold a candle to crawling around on the grass looking for ladybugs. I sold my company, and although things had not gone as I had planned them, I eased into my new role, and I was energized. I left the traditional career world and never looked back. I have never regretted my decision for one moment.

"I jumped in with everything I had, you name it, and we tried it! Music, ballet, art classes, fairy school. Park dates, cookie-making dates, and yes, scrapbooking. I made new friends, the moms of Annabelle's friends. When she started preschool, I joined committees, signed up for bake sales, book fairs, room mom, teacher appreciation lunches, stuffing envelopes, driving to field trips . . . there was no task too small or time commitment too big. At one point I overheard my daughter tell a complete stranger, 'My mommy works at my school, she plans everything!' Okay, so maybe I had gone slightly overboard. I saw many other women selling screen-plays, traveling, getting promotions, yet I did not question my choice and was not feeling 'left behind.'

"I do have a confession: As comfortable as I felt with my choice and the rhythm our lives had taken, I have had many days when I felt like a walking cliché. I have had lengthy conversations, border-ing on heated debates, about My Gym vs. Gymboree, minivan vs. mini minivan, cheese sticks, apple slices, juice boxes, and eating sand. I have sung songs with the words *chicken fricassee* and *choo choo* in the same sentence.

"Did I need more? Was I feeling unfulfilled? No, but my identity had shifted. I was Annabelle and Emet's mom. In my new, self-appointed job, I began to feel like a volun-told, not a volun-teer. It wasn't as though I was having conscious feelings of discontent and restlessness, but I think this is when I realized another shift was happening. It was becoming clear to me that at some point I would find something that excited me enough to want to re-engage outside the boundaries of being 'Mom.'

"I realized that the time I spent in service to my children and their school was not the only way to express my commitment to my family. Much of the time I spent selling school carnival tickets did not really make me a better mother, friend, or wife. At the time, I did not know another way to express that commitment. When I heard about Vodvil, a restaurant venture that sounded completely new and interesting, and that done right could be a huge hit, I realized that's what I should be doing. That was how I would have an identity apart from my family.

"I don't have a label for the 'refreshed' me. I do not believe I have carved a new niche for myself or discovered untapped re-sources I never knew I had. I haven't found a new calling. I am just taking all the experiences, learning, and growth of the past eight years and bringing them to something new.

"There are two things I have learned in this process of 'reinvention.' The first is that traditional thinking doesn't always work for me. I need to do what I know in my heart is good for my family and me, even when others question and judge my decisions. In doing this I also teach my children a valuable lesson—that other people's opinions of me are none of my business. The second thing is that overly enmeshing with my children is not good. Of course I do not want my children to feel any pain or hardship, but it can be a healthy way to learn to navigate life. It is possible to be overly connected to them. They need to know where I end and they begin.

"Do not think that even though you have redefined your life as a mother, this is the only path to walk. I hope I will forever refresh, reinvent. I don't know where this road will lead next, as this is just the beginning of this journey."

Kabrel shows us that there doesn't have to be something wrong or missing to reinvent. Hers is a prime example of AND. She loves her family life, and she is also finding something for herself.

THE JOURNEY AWAITS

Remember that above all else, it takes courage to reinvent. The other side can be like nothing you ever experienced before, but that is a good thing. Just know that as you move through this quest, we can assure you without reservation that as a mom, you are beyond capable. Look at what you do in your day right now. If anyone can do this, it's you.

Jen

I didn't reinvent gracefully for a while, and my relationship with my husband turned into marital chaos. I felt guilty about wanting to make a change, and that guilt sparked marital issues, and a lot of sadness and confusion. It didn't have to be like that.

The feeling that something has to change is real. You have to address it, with everyone in your life. Reinvention is not always easy. There may be stresses and strains along the way. Some may be new, some may have been buried beneath the surface for years, only to spring up when changing your life starts to change the lives of others. It's okay. You're going to make it through and come out better than ever, even with your partner.

NOW YOU KNOW

You thought this juggling act you're doing daily was tough. Now you see you might need to stop doing all you've been doing, and that much of the pressure you're feeling may indeed be self-imposed because of your expectations of yourself and what you feel are the expectations of others. Here's what else you have learned:

- You're not going to have the same life you had before you were a mother. Don't fight the changes; embrace them.
- There are only twenty-four hours in every day; with your role as mother, most of these will be taken up by your family. Don't fritter away the only precious minutes you have to yourself by feeling sorry for yourself. Let go of the guilt.
- It's okay to say no—and okay to say it often.
- You now have a self-evaluation questionnaire to work on to start figuring it all out—so get started!
- If you don't reinvent or stake your claim, you risk existing without really living.

Chapter 3

Reinvent *with* Your Family
Getting Your House in Order

I was four years into being a stay-at-home mom. Though I was still enjoying the kids and glad I had given the past few years to them, I was starting to get restless. There were times when my husband and I were out, and I felt that everyone else had such interesting things to talk about, while all I could add was an uh huh or oh yeah. The proverbial straw for me, however, came on a random Saturday morning. I lay in bed with my kids watching some inane cartoon while my husband was in the other room paying bills. He didn't tell me that he was paying bills, but I could tell from the audible grunts, moans, and f-bombs he was throwing around.

I casually walked in to inform him that the kids could hear him, when he laid into me, "This Mastercard bill is out of control!" he yelled. "What in the world is this Picket Fences bill?" I looked at this enraged stranger in my house and calmly stated that most of the expenses were his work expenses, which had been reimbursed, and that the outrageous random purchase from Picket Fences was the coat he bought me for Mother's Day!

That was it. I decided right then and there that I would not feel like a child being reprimanded for purchases that I didn't even make, and that

I had to take that stress for both of us out of the equation. I needed to
bring money in again, but how?

I didn't like the feeling of being controlled financially, that was the
end of the line for me. It lit a fire in me. It was clear whatever we were
doing wasn't working. I needed to be doing something, for myself and
for the household, and from that point, I started looking. Yes, I needed to
start bringing in some money, but I knew that though I wanted to work, I
didn't want to work full time or go back to my old job. I wanted to be
there for my kids, but how could I possibly do both? I was really confused.

—Jen

Exactly how the realization hits that it's time for a change is different for all of us. For some, like Jen, it strikes in the midst of a heat-
edly dramatic situation. There's an immediately identifiable cause,
and the effect is our reaction. After months of having the feeling
of something not being quite right, it only takes a moment to see
clearly, finally, that a change is needed—and what that change
might be. For others, the realization is gradual, unfolding over
months or even years as a yearning for something more. We're
happy in our lives, but we feel we could be happier. We open our
eyes and our minds—and when we're able, our schedules—to possibilities, and when the right one hits us, when something really
starts to make sense more than ever before, we go after it.

As mothers, we can't expect that we'll move from realization
to reinvention overnight. It does takes months or even years because of the limits we have on our time. For many of us, knowing
that we need the change is one thing; actually finding the time to
figure out what it is and set it in motion is pretty much where we
run into trouble.

Elizabeth Gilbert's *Eat, Pray, Love* relates her need to rediscover herself. Although she lamented being alone at first, it gave
her the opportunity to take a journey of self-discovery on a real

journey—an extended vacation. Single and free, the whole world was open to her, and she was able to take advantage of the fact that nothing was tying her down. But what if she had two or three kids to contend with? Would an exploration such as hers have been feasible? Would it have been even remotely possible?

Imagine the mental clarity you could have if you could just "leave" for a couple of weeks, a month—or a year. Just to spend some time focusing on you and figuring things out. Well of course that isn't going to happen. So what can you do?

As it is, most days we lack the mental clarity to even construct a useful grocery list, with all the clatter and clamoring that goes on around us. How are we supposed to devise a reinvention strategy as we raise our kids and keep even a semblance of order in our lives while we're at it? The thing is, we can't do it without help—and those we need to help us most are the ones we help the most: our partners and children. We need to involve them in our reinventions, and in this chapter, we're going to help you figure out how.

MOTHER OF REINVENTION:
BETSY (PART 2)

Navigating with Your Spouse

BETSY BROWN BRAUN, sixty-three, married forty years, three kids (triplets, age thirty-three)

BEST ADVICE: *The nature of your relationship with a husband or partner has everything to do with how you parent.*

"Being married forty years is a pretty darn satisfying and mystifying experience. In this day and age, when divorce is more and more common and acceptable, forty years sounds almost impossible. I can't imagine raising triplets with a husband who isn't hands-on. But as it happens, my husband is an easygoing, amenable, great sport sort of a guy. He is the perfect complement to me—high energy, directed, and bossy!

"The nature of your relationship with your husband or partner has everything to do with how you parent. As I have said over and over, people whose emotional houses are in order, who are not issue filled, will raise kids who will be just fine. Unbalanced partnerships lead to unhappy relationships, and that almost always manifests in your children's behavior.

"My support system was my family; they have always been my cheerleaders. But more than anyone, my husband has completely supported me and cheered me on in every single endeavor, whether my paintings or writing. He is my biggest fan and supporter.

"We have reinvented ourselves as a couple many different times. Now, with three married children, we are doing it again, backing off and watching our kids build their own nests. And hopefully, soon we will reinvent ourselves as a couple again as grandparents. Have we reached our potential as a couple? Who knows! But we do continue to evolve."

Betsy understands that the most important support system is your family. Clearly, her success in her career has so much to do with her success in her marriage and with her family.

GEARING UP

Are you up for the task? Can you really manage a reinvention and a family? Well, think about it. Isn't it you who's able to stay on top of everyone getting their homework done while you make dinner and tend to countless other tasks throughout the day and into the night? Aren't you the woman who manages to get two or three very stubborn small people out the door in time for the school bus most mornings? Wasn't it you sitting on the bathroom floor in the middle of the night that time, breast-feeding your infant in one arm while you held and hugged and comforted your other child, who was vomiting his guts out all over the bathroom and you and his little sister? And who cleaned it all up and did all that laundry before your husband got up for work the next morning?

Yes, that's you. You have risen to the occasion again and again when the needs of those you love needed to be filled. Now you need to remember that you, too, are a person you love, and you need to rise to meet your own needs. And just as you have gone the extra mile and made sacrifices to help your family, so too can they rise and help you. They're just going to need prompting from you.

Jen

During the initial stages of our reinvention, Barb and I spent most of our time planning while having play dates together. One of us would bring her kids over to the other's house and between feeding, taking care of, and watching the kids (yes, there were a few free moments), we brainstormed about ways we wanted our lives to look, how we wanted to make other women feel they weren't alone, how we wanted to do something together. It is amazing that anything got accomplished, but we made it happen by finding those small windows of opportunity and knowing where we were in our lives with small children who needed our time and love. It was multitasking at its best, and we made it work. You can make it work, too. You just have to think outside the box.

Our desire to help other mothers stemmed from our experience and empathy for those going through what we were going through.

Talking to other women, I realized that many were feeling inadequate in either their mothering or juggling all their tasks or their relationships—or all of the above. This realization made me want to do something to help. We thought it would be great to create a forum in which we, and our audience, could find the answers together.

MOTHER OF REINVENTION: RISA (PART 2)

RISA GREEN, thirty-eight, married twelve years, two kids (ages eight and six)

BEST ADVICE: *See what piques your interest, what gets you all excited inside. It's not worth making a change and upheaving your whole life unless you are going to love what you do.*

"After my first child was born, I worked out a deal with the head of a school whereby I worked as a college counselor. I could work at home two days a week, which was a great compromise because it allowed me to spend time with my daughter. After two years of that, it was made clear to me that after my next maternity leave, I would have to go back to five days in the office. I was very torn, because I loved my job very much, but the idea of going back to work full time and not getting those two days a week anymore with my daughter was really devastating.

"During my first maternity leave I'd written a collection of essays about pregnancy and motherhood, and I'd gotten an agent who was trying to sell it. About a year after my first child was born, my agent told me that the book wasn't selling as it was, but that the feedback she'd received was that I should rewrite it as a novel. I really didn't want to do that at first. I had a day job and a one-year-old, but my agent pushed and told me I would always be sorry if I didn't at least try.

"It was really, really, hard. On my in-office days, I worked all day, then I came home and played with my daughter and gave her dinner and bathed her and played with her again until bedtime, and then I would write from 9:00 p.m. until one in the morning. It was exhausting, and I was crabby all the time and I barely spent any time with my husband. Then my agent called and told me that she had sold the book based on a partial submission, and they wanted to make a two-book deal for this book and a sequel. A few weeks later she made the same deal with an Italian publisher, and all of the deals together equaled my salary for the next year. I begged my husband to let me quit my job and pursue writing full time. I loved doing it very much, and I had never had more fun doing anything in my entire life. Although it was a little stressful worrying about where the money would come from next year, my husband was completely supportive, and I think he was just really happy and relieved that I had found something I enjoyed that also paid.

"My husband helps more than most husbands, but not as much as he probably could. He has his own business, so his work time is flexible, and he drives the kids to school once a week, coaches some of their sports teams, and takes them to games and practices. He's home most nights by six, so we eat dinner together, and he helps with their baths and bedtime. He also deals with a lot of house stuff, like getting things fixed or hiring a gardener. But I do the bulk of the kids' stuff. I don't think he has expectations of me per se, but he expects certain things to be done. He doesn't care whether I do it or outsource it to someone else, but he's not going to do it.

"I am in a really good place right now. I write a weekly column, which keeps me connected to my audience while I'm working on a new book, and now that both of my kids are (finally) in school full time, I feel that I have a fairly regular, daily work schedule, and it's really good for me to feel I have a purpose. I don't really regret anything or wish that I'd done anything differently."

What we learn from Risa is she came with a plan with her husband. She didn't quit her job until she had secured the income needed for her family.

NOT EVERYTHING IS YOUR RESPONSIBILITY

Your reinvention definitely requires an understanding with your husband and your kids, because everyone's roles in your household will need to be tweaked. All of you will be affected. Some of your time will have to be allocated differently. Everyone will definitely have to be on board.

Of course, that doesn't mean it will be easy for anyone, or even apparent to your husband and children all the time. As we're taking our "time out" to sit and write this book, one of our husbands has just barged in on us to let us know he can't pick up the kids from school later. Of course we (one of us and the unnamed husband) had a fight. And just as all this was happening, the school nurse called and informed us that one of our kids needed to be picked up right away. Can you guess who was immediately nominated for that task? Here we are trying to get our work done; that doesn't mean he sees that clearly. All he sees is that the mother, the default parent, is home and breathing and therefore should be the one to pick up the kids.

The default parent seems to always be the mother. It's definitely unfair to say it's all our "fault" that this happens. But we definitely see things differently than our husbands do when it comes to matters of the home. They don't realize that a cabinet door once opened also needs to be closed, or that there isn't a magical force that lifts dropped dirty socks off the floor. There's really no clear-cut scientific explanation for why they don't hear babies crying in the night or why having a routine and sticking to it is actually important for a kid. When their children, who usually eat dinner at six, are acting up at the dinner table at seven-thirty when the husbands finally get around to feeding them, those husbands think the children are just being bad. And of course they are—but husbands don't really see that they've had anything to do with it. Most of them just don't know.

Jen

I did a lot of talking with my husband about my desire to create the show with Barb. While I was talking, he seemed supportive, but that didn't come through in his actions. Even though he was telling me that he was excited for me that I was excited about something, he still wanted the same version of the wife and mother that I was, and it took awhile to work on rebalancing the equation. We're still working on it.

Your husband may not like hearing some of the things you need to tell him, but he has to be told. As much as we would like people to read our minds, they just can't. By spelling out what you are going through and what your plan is, you are setting everything up for much more success and happiness. Also, be sure you listen to him, too. Your husband may also be going through his own set of changes and also has needs and a plan. Get together on your plan, and you can work it out together.

On top of that, you're going to have to learn to let go sometimes and let him do things his way when you're not around. If you make the experience of his taking over some things unpleasant, he's not going to be as available as you may want or need him to be in your reinvention. We discuss more about talking to your partner and kids as we move through this chapter.

DO YOU AND YOUR SPOUSE PARENT DIFFERENTLY?

You are going to need your husband's help in all of this, so it's important that you not micromanage him, or he will definitely not want to help you. You may think he is going to completely mess up your kids or neglect them by watching the game, or they are going to get hurt because men just don't pay attention to detail the way moms do. Remember, you need him on board with you. Make him want to be on board with you.

Says parenting expert and author Betsy Brown Braun,

Co-parenting doesn't mean you are going to agree on everything you do. It means you are going to take turns parenting. Children need to learn how to relate to different people. It's part of emotional intelligence and social intelligence. It is actually really healthy for kids to live with parents who have different parenting styles. If you have some correcting to do, you are allowed to talk about it with your spouse but not in front of your children. Everything you do in front of your children with your co-parent your children are taking it in. They observe how you talk to him and how he talks to you. Children will do what they see, not what you say. So you are modeling relationships and how people get along.

See, ladies: You are doing your kids a favor by letting your husband help out (even if you think he is not doing it right).

MOTHER OF REINVENTION: ANNE (PART 1)

Roles and Regulating

ANNE TRACY EMERSON, forty, married for sixteen years, two kids (ages ten and five)

BEST ADVICE: *Find a balance in your household that works for you—it doesn't matter what other people do.*

"I married a man who can cook like a dream and entertain a room full of people. After living with him for more than twenty years, I know what he excels in—and I also know what he should never be allowed to touch. One of those things is laundry.

"We're both most comfortable with me being at home with the children. We've switched the roles before, and it didn't work for us. Maybe it has worked for other people, but we're good at what we're good at, and that's how we run our house. I do a majority of the cleaning, and Patrick helps tremendously. I handle a majority of the childcare, and again, Patrick jumps in and helps as his job permits. When I have to go away for a few days, he steps in beautifully and probably works harder at entertaining them than I do. If I have a long-term project, one he can't cover for, I hire someone to help out. I don't ask him to pick up the pieces on a long-term basis, because he likes to work, it makes him happy, and why would I discourage that?

"If there is a place we're still working on getting the balance right, it's when one of us has a project that bleeds into 'family time.' It doesn't happen all the time, but at least a few times a year, things get out of whack. That's okay. We both accept it and work through it. That's a really important part of our marriage: Flexibility."

We love that Anne understands who her husband is, where he ex-cels, and what his limitations are. We could all use a lesson in that. It would help all our marriages.

LET GO, LET GROW

If the responsibility for taking care of the children always falls on you, how are you ever going to find time to reinvent? Finding time for yourself has to be scheduled. As we talked about in the last chapter, as you start feeling your way through it, taking baby steps, you'll see the opportunities. You're going to impress your-self by how creative you can be.

You've realized there's a void in your life, and you've spent time trying to identify what the void is. Now is the time for you to start taking concrete steps to start moving toward fulfillment. Remember, no matter how others (and, incidentally, yourself) may try to make you feel about it, this is not selfish. Your re-invention will do wonders for you, which will in turn make you a better mother, wife, and woman. Not only will your family bene-fit, but so will your employees, your friends, and anyone you in-teract with over the course of a day. You'll have happiness and fulfillment lighting your soul, and it will shine out of you to en-lighten and enrich others. This is truly a universal win-win, but it probably won't seem that way to anyone at first.

How badly do you want this reinvention? We're going to be honest with you here: You're going to be met with resistance in many different ways and even from many different people—and that includes yourself.

We mentioned in previous chapters that you're going to have to let go of your guilt and your expectations. You also have to ease up on your expectations of others. If you're going to call on your mother to take your kids for a few hours in the evening, you'll have to take a deep breath and accept that she might let them watch *The Bachelor* and feed them chocolate even when they haven't finished their dinners. You'll have to accept that if your kids don't eat lunch or dinner on time when left with your husband, they are not going to die. They may be obnoxious, but at least for the time being, that's his problem, not yours.

You are probably going to have to fight with your husband from time to time and even incur some level of judgment from your family. But that doesn't matter. You have to keep striving, for yourself and in spite of yourself. It's not going to be easy, especially when you're probably outnumbered by people who have been enjoying the status quo at your expense. They are going to fight the change, and you are going to fight back, but learn to do it in a way that increases the love and connection, not destroys it. Your reinvention has to be as necessary to you as blood and breath, and you have to treat it that way.

Jen

It's taken a long time to re-create our roles in the family. My husband's view was that I did drop-off and pickup from school and got dinner on the table, that I was available to him when he needed me, and that I was available to be the at-home parent when the kids were home from school. Essentially, he wanted me to have what I wanted, but he wanted to keep everything he already had. I wanted to tell him what he really needed was two wives, but instead I just kept talking it through with him, calmly. Okay, sometimes not so calmly, but I tried! I told him that I was overwhelmed, that I was taking on too much and needed his assistance. At my worst, I snapped at him (and still do), but I realized that that got me nowhere. The reinvention and the changes are happening, but slowly. He didn't immediately embrace how things were going to be, and I had to take a deep breath and a step back and not get frustrated when things weren't happening as fast as I wanted them to.

MONEY MATTERS

No one likes to talk about money, but we all have bills to pay. Your reinvention may have an effect on your finances if, for example, you're looking to work fewer hours to be with your kids or you want to start a business that has some initial start-up costs. It is imperative that you take a close look at your finances and figure out where the "wiggle room" is, if any, just as you are doing with your time.

If you are married, sit down with your spouse and get a clear idea of what your current budget is, what you need, and where you can cut back. We are sure that like most people, you are reading this and thinking, cut back? I can barely make it as it is. We understand. Don't let that discourage your reinvention. You are going to have to work within your finances. We promise you that you can still successfully reinvent, find something that you are passionate about, and make ends meet.

"Nobody knows how to talk about money," says Dr. Bonnie Eiker Weil, a family therapist and author of *Financial Infidelity*. "It's a breeding ground for a power struggle. Most people don't talk about money because they don't know how or they don't want to get their partner angry or hurt. Here are some things to remember when it comes to money and your relationship:

Money comes second; the relationship should come first.
With today's economic climate, money skills are more important than ever.
Whoever makes the money should not be controlling the money.

"An honest, open dialogue with your spouse regarding both of your spending can help create a healthy, happy relationship now," she says, "and a safer financial future."

Reinvent Your Family:
This Is About All of You

Although your reinvention is yours and yours alone, how you make it happen is not just about you. There are others to consider. You have to pay attention to how your actions affect everyone in your family. Yes, you need a change, but you have to see this change within the context of the "big picture." You are indeed looking for something for yourself, but other people are involved, and you need to think about them also as you move along.

There is a "me" in marriage; it's what keeps it together—the M on one end, the E on the other. If you disregard the "me," it all falls apart.

You already know that something's not working for you, and you've started to pull the pieces together to figure out what that is. Now it's time to get your partner on board as you begin your reinvention. In our cases, by partners, we mean husbands.

Jen

I wasn't thinking about how hard it was for my husband, how all the financial pressure was on him. He was a young man with a lot of responsibility, and it affected how he dealt with me and the children.

But we do know that there are many partners women rely on to help raise kids, and we'll discuss some of these other figures later in the chapter.

In any situation, communication is key—and this situation is no different. No one in your family is going to notice you sulking and try to draw out of you what's troubling you and how they can make it better. (Well, maybe your own mother would do that, but it's not likely to come from your eight-year-old. And even if your husband is super-sensitive, it's not going to come from him, either.)

Start with your husband. Be sure you have all your ducks in a row when you do, and assure him that your need for reinvention is not about him or that he's wrong for spending his time the way he does. Be as clear and specific as possible. Make sure he knows this is a *positive change* for the family. Discuss with him first where you need his help and what you have in mind for the children. Then, together, decide how you're going to present the reinvention to your family. He's your biggest ally in all of this. You have to make sure he's prepared to get your back for you, and that you can address the situation with the children as a team.

Don't let him think that you're ungrateful or resentful. He wants validation that he's doing a good job as a husband and father. Men love praise. If you praise him, it will make all the difference in the world. If you're not fighting with your husband, kudos to you—you're better than us! However, chances are that if you're looking for this reinvention, you probably are fighting with your husband.

Remember that your husband is adjusting, too, even if it's not in the same way you are. Men don't normally stop working to raise a family, so they are still receiving validation through the channels they always have; they don't need it in the same way a woman does. Also, society does not put the "expectations" of caring for a family on the man. Perfect example: A dad is in Starbucks carrying his child in a Baby Bjorn. Everyone thinks how cute he is, and what a wonderful dad! Nobody looks at a mother that way. Of course she's expected to be with her baby. (And if she isn't with her baby at that moment, she could even be judged as being a bad mom.)

Since you became parents, his life and yours have been permanently altered. He was used to getting your undivided attention. He was the one you used to nurture. He has growing pains and adjustment issues, just as you do. When he walks through the front door at night, he's not returning to the same partner he once knew. Long ago, you were happy to see him when he came home at night, and now the overwhelming responsibilities of motherhood often leave you resenting him. Remember, he also enjoyed the days when you were happy to see him. This is a two-way street.

No matter how frustrating things are with your husband in this situation, he's not the problem. Just because he's not doing all the things you want him to, just as you want him to, doesn't mean he's not supporting what you're doing or is standing in the way of your reinvention. In fact, you need him on your side now more than ever. **When you look at your husband, don't assume he's part of the problem; see him as part of the solution.**

Everyone needs to be validated: you, your spouse, and your kids. Don't get so caught up in what you are feeling that you forget to tend to the needs of your family. Remember to commend your children for helping around the house or thank your husband for putting the kids to bed so you can go out with a girl-friend. A little validation and thanks go a long way.

MOTHER OF REINVENTION: RENEE

From Retail to Real Estate

RENEE AVEDON, married, two kids (ages nineteen and sixteen)

BEST ADVICE: *Take a risk and follow your dreams. Transition and change can be difficult, but by exploring different avenues you can experience fulfillment and personal success. Failure to try lasts forever.*

"My husband and I had run our store, Avedon, now located in Beverly Hills, together since 1984. We got married in 1990 and shortly thereafter welcomed our first child, and I became a stay-at-home, full-time mom. My second was born three years later.

"I had always been a career-oriented person, so being a full-time mom was a very new experience for me. It took a lot of adjusting on my part, because I really didn't have a mother figure to ask advice from. I read a lot of books on parenting and winged it raising my kids, and I am fortunate to have a very supportive husband and mother-in-law who helped! I don't think I could have done it alone.

"When my kids were old enough not to need me full time I wanted to take on something new: to fulfill my secret dream of selling real estate. My husband was on board. He told me he thought I would do well and encouraged me. My kids were also very supportive about me starting a new career. Within six months of getting my license, I had sold $12 million worth of real estate.

"I didn't realize how much of my time and energy real estate would take up, so it took some getting used to by everyone. All of a sudden, all of my time and energy was going toward my clients, and my husband felt a little neglected. It took a bit of an adjustment. We soon worked it out, and with time, everyone got used to it. I was also fortunate to have my husband's mother as well as close friends and relatives helping out. I believe it takes 'a village' to successfully raise a well-rounded child.

"My husband always attended all of the main school events, and I knew if I needed him to cover for me and carpool, I could count on him. We met when we were in high school and quite literally grew up together. Though we may not always agree on everything, we both understand that being able to compromise and having mutual respect play a big part in keeping a harmonious marriage.

"As my children embark on their own journeys, I find myself continuing to search for more personal fulfillment, professionally and personally. Both parenting and life are journeys that can never be mastered. We will always have some regrets, but one must persevere and always remember that happiness is a state of mind that can grow and live under any condition!"

Renee exemplifies being malleable as she went through her re-invention. Although she was thrilled to have her new real estate business thriving, she also understood that her family was being affected and made the adjustments she needed to.

POWER STRUGGLES—KEEPING THEM UNDER CONTROL

We've all had those moments when our partner tries to tell us what to do, as if that person knows better than we do. And when it happens, it makes smoke come out of our ears. But there are two ways of handling things. Yes, one way is to lash out, to interpret what the other person has to say as an attack on your competency and strike back. The other is to take a step back and take control of the situation without losing your patience. **The decision is in your hands whether you are going to ignite or diffuse the situation.**

Part of the reason we struggle with our spouses over the division of domestic duties is because,

> Barb (only half-laughing)
> Don't even talk to your husband about anything you need or want from him without having sex with him first.

as we said before, men are different than we are. They don't take the initiative in matters having to do with the children, because that's not who they are. "Men are connectable by instruction," says Dr. Bonnie Eaker Weil. "They need to be told what to do," but not overly so. She explains that this is "because they can only take approximately thirty seconds of us talking before they shut down and tune out." Just because you need a change doesn't mean you're going to be able to flip a switch and change your partner. You're not asking him to change who he is; you're asking him to try to work with you. You're looking for solutions here, not a brand new husband. Tell him what you need and see if he can accommodate you. If he can't, don't explode. There are other solutions out there.

GETTING YOUR HOUSE IN ORDER

It's impossible to reinvent when your home base isn't in order. It's like trying to get your work done at a messy, disorganized desk, or making dinner in a messy kitchen. Yeah, you could muddle through and try to make it work despite the chaos, but it would have been so much easier if you had the workspace in order to begin with.

Reinvention is the same. You need to get your house in order if you're going to be creating something new there. Just as you're not going to have a successful meal if you don't have the proper ingredients and right tools, so also are you not going to be able to pull off a successful reinvention in a climate of chaos.

Think of all the time you're wasting when you wake up every morning and end up dodging bullets all day. If you wake up without a plan, without things set in place and ready to be set in motion, you're just going to be reacting to everything that happens, and as a result, spinning your wheels.

Reinvent Your Family: Don't React, Plan

To get your house in order, you need to get your family on board. **If your marriage is in a state of constant challenge, you will not be able to reinvent.** If your whole life is like herding cats, when are you going to have the time to devote to you? Get organized, and you'll conserve plenty of energy that you can put in the "reinvention reserve."

Sit down at the beginning of each week and make a schedule. Look at what you have going on and decide then and there who's picking up the kids, who's picking up the dry cleaning, who's in charge of dinner from one day to the next. Create a timetable you can agree on. If someone on the "team" has a busier schedule than usual in the coming week, the schedule has to reflect the others pitching in and picking up the slack.

SAMPLE CHORE CHART—FOR JEN'S KIDS, COOPER AND LILAH

Feel free to use this as a guide or an inspiration to develop a timetable that works best for your family.

	Mon	Tues	Wed	Thurs	Fri	Sat	Sun
Get mail	C	L	C	L	C	L	
Clean Room	C&L	C&L	C&L	C&L	C&L	C&L	
Set Table	L	C	L	C	L	C	
Clear Table	C&L	C&L	C&L	C&L	C&L	C&L	
Empty trashcans	C	L	C	L	C	L	
Lay out clothes	C&L	C&L	C&L	C&L	C&L	C&L	

When we first talked all this through with our husbands, we don't think they really understood, on paper, just how much the responsibilities would be shifting. In fact, we didn't even realize how much the roles in our houses were going to be altered. Even with the schedules in place, there's still some daily negotiation over who does what, but at least we have a guideline now. The first thing we did was talk with our husbands about the bare minimum we needed them to do to free up some of our time for our reinvention, and on the weeks that we stick to it—or at least close to it—there isn't a lot of bitterness or resentment that one person has to do everything.

The schedule is as important for your partner as it is for you, and, in some ways, it's more important for him. As we said, men don't operate with a laundry list of to-do's. They need prompting. If there's a plan in place, your partner has a guideline to follow. If he can't do his tasks for a day—maybe he had to work late or has an unexpected meeting—at least what needs to be covered is on paper, and other arrangements can be made more easily.

When you create the schedule, be sure to keep your expectations realistic. Explain what you need and open a discussion to work together on getting the tasks done. Everyone likes to be needed. Don't underestimate the power of the word *need* in your vocabulary. Don't "ask" him to do things on certain days; his help in all of this is not optional, and saying "would you mind" makes it seem optional. **Your reinvention is not a luxury; it is a necessity.** Even though times have changed, and women are educated and also work, there's still a perception that women will do the heavy lifting at home, and that is probably not going to change. You have to establish parameters so that it looks like the home responsibilities are more shared, and that you're doing all this to help each other meet the expectations and demands of the household.

Remember, the goal of this exercise is to find the time you need to reinvent. If your husband isn't willing or able to share in these responsibilities, don't think you are stuck. It is time to get creative. Do not give up.

Reinvent Your Family: You Are the CEO

You have needs that need to be met, but don't expect that the schedule is going to be some magical document that will change your husband completely. Yes, it will help for him to see the whole scope of things that need to be done all spelled out like that, but if your husband doesn't do laundry, don't expect that he's magically going to start because the schedule suggests he should.

Jen

For the longest time, I got so mad at my husband if lights were out around the house or things were broken. I had this expectation that as the man, these were his responsibilities. I finally realized (and it has taken me more than a decade) that he hates these tasks as much as I do. I now have a wonderful handyman, and he's worth every penny.

Barb

In my house, we divided and conquered: We took the list of things that needed to be done, literally divided it between us based on what we were good at—or at least better at—and what we liked to do—or didn't dislike doing as much as something else. I'm an awful cook, so my husband's in charge of the kitchen. He's also in charge of his own laundry, and of pickups and drop-offs on his assigned days.

The way that I find best for running my family is that I am the CEO of our house—just as my husband is the CEO of his company—and he needs to follow my lead. I know this might sound horrifying to some of you, but that's how it works best for us, and it might also for other families. Men like to know what is expected of them; they work in specifics. They don't want to guess about what they're supposed to be doing. If you want to get the best result from your husband, manage him like an employee. Men want to know that they did a good job; they want to be validated. Praise your husband, don't criticize him. Micromanaging your husband will not get you the right result!

Look for options outside the household and have your "safeties" in place. Maybe you can build into your schedule that you send your child to daycare for three hours a day, or create a "buddy system" with another parent for watching each other's kids. Each partner has to be flexible in this. Things pop up in your lives all the time that will try you and trip you up from following the schedule, and you just have to roll with it—both of you. You need to be flexible and find compromise.

Reinvent Your Family:
Stop Fighting, Start Communicating

We've all made the mistake of speaking too harshly at one time or another, and it never helps the situation. Don't be nasty with your partner, even if you're angry with him for not meeting those pesky expectations of yours. How you speak and the tone you use are just as important as the words you say.

Dr. Bonnie Eaker Weil

"Mother Nature picks the person that is going to give you the most trouble. You don't want to get rid of that person, you just have to remember that that power struggle is going to take you to real life love."

The next time you fight, think about how much time and energy you are wasting. Fighting sucks the energy right out of you, and you need all the energy you can possibly spare to reinvent.

THE PATH OF RESISTANCE

Reinvention hasn't been easy for us. We've fought hard to fit our needs into marriage and a family situation that works for everyone. It's not easy, but it's worth it. Once it does start working, it gets easier. Both of us faced challenging times in our marriages.

Changing how things were done did shake things up. There were plenty of power struggles over who does what and when.

Jen

My husband travels often for work. When he leaves, he just rolls out with his suitcase in hand and poof! he's gone. When I go out of town for work, I leave behind numerous documents providing my travel information, emergency numbers, and where the kids need to be and when. Basically, I leave a breakdown of what each day looks like from morning till night. I'm not going to lie; it bothers me, but I don't think this is going to change. Sometimes we have to choose our battles, and this is not one of the ones I choose.

Barb

My husband and I had worked out a schedule wherein I would work from 6:00 a.m. to 9:00 a.m., and he would watch the kids. Then he would go to work at 9:00 a.m., and the kids would become my responsibility.

One day I had a big conference call with a client, and I reminded my husband I could not be disturbed, so I went into my home office and locked the door. About ten minutes into the call I heard banging on the door and "Mommy! Mommy! Mommy!" Where was my husband?

I tried to ignore the kids and keep talking, but then there was more banging, and it sounded like kicking and screaming and crying. Of course at this point I wasn't listening to one word of the conference call, but I was starting to get worried about what was going on outside the office. Where was my husband?

The call finally finished, and I ran out of my office, to find my twin daughters screaming on the floor at the top of their lungs. "Where's Daddy?" I asked. Then I looked up, to see my husband sitting at his computer, with his headphones on. It was clear he had no respect for me and my work, and things needed to change immediately. Just because my office was in the house didn't mean that my job was not as important as his!

While you're navigating motherhood and being a wife and reinventing, there are going to be a million variables spinning around, and you are not going to be able to have a handle on all of them. **Control only what you can control, and let go of what you can't.**

Reinvent Your Family: Control Only What You Can Control

You can't control how your husband perceives what goes on in your day, just as you can't perceive his. So if you need a pat on the back, give it to yourself. Congratulating yourself for finding fulfillment is something you can control. If you expect validation (there's that word again!) from others, you may just be setting yourself up for disappointment.

Barb

Throughout your reinvention, you will find different levels of partnership with your husband. When we started out, my husband and I were pretty much equal. For a while, it didn't feel like we were equal anymore. I felt the load of the responsibilities were much heavier on my side. But now that I've been at this for awhile, I know he has way more respect for me, and our relationship is more equal again. I think he even "likes" me more because I'm happy. Because I figured out what I wanted and I went after it.

A lot of women are soon going to say, "Here's what I want to do, and my husband is not supporting it" because they expect two things: that their husbands will follow their instructions to the letter and that their husbands will initiate ways to help. As we talked about in this chapter, this expectation might not be realistic. It's not just your husband, it's all husbands! Men are just not programmed that way. Expecting more than your partner can deliver will create problems, which will only add another barrier to your getting what you need. Discuss what's needed, agree together on what can be accomplished, and don't expect more than what's agreed on.

The other issue you may have with your husband is that he doesn't quite get what you're doing, especially if you're exploring a direction you've never explored before. If you have no background in art but tell your husband you want to open an art gallery, he's going to be suspicious. Take baby steps—for you and for him. Start small. If opening an art gallery is what you really want to do, start by maybe contacting a couple of artists and having a show at your house. You need to get your feet wet and also his. The more accustomed to the idea he becomes, the more comfortable and confident he'll be. And that goes for you, too. You don't need to jump right into a giant endeavor. Try it out on a smaller scale and get yourself used to the idea. Build confidence and skills before you branch out and grow.

If you are married, it's unlikely that your husband is going to be very excited to pick up extra responsibility around the house. Be prepared for his reaction and try not to freak out. Just because you've come to this realization doesn't mean you can make him see it right away. It may take him a little while to get with the program, and by a little while, in some cases we mean years. Just keep restating how important this is to you, and work with him to try to make it work.

MOTHER OF REINVENTION: CANDICE (PART 1)

CANDICE PATE, thirty-six, married seven years, two kids (ages three and five)

BEST ADVICE: *Have faith that your reinvention will work itself out. It's a process.*

"My husband was very supportive as I worked through what I wanted to do and has tried to pitch in. He's been very supportive of me emotionally, though there is some frustration from my end feeling like all the kids' stuff still falls in my lap. Ten percent of my time is spent figuring out creative childcare solutions! I still shoulder all of the responsibilities in the home that I did when I was a full-time mom (and that was my only job). Though he is getting better about pitching in, that's definitely been a source of frustration. The kids don't seem any worse for the wear, and my time with them now is more meaningful, focused.

"He is a very involved dad, and the kids are crazy about him. He is not as involved in the day-to-day workings of the household, however. Ninety percent of the cleaning, bill-paying, and sitter-hiring stuff falls on my plate. That was okay when I was at home full time—it felt fair to me—but with my going back to work, the negotiation has begun.

HANG TIGHT

If your husband has an adverse reaction when you tell him you need to reinvent, you may think you want to leave him. We want you to stay. His ego may be bruised, and it could take awhile for him to understand that this is not about him, it's about you.

We've said in the beginning of this chapter and throughout the book that we come at this situation from the same place: We are longtime married women intent on staying married. For that reason, our advice is always to try to stay together—to work things out. There are times when full cooperation isn't feasible, but for the most part, if you make a commitment to work things out together, you can make it together.

> **Jen**
>
> I thought I had the perfect family, but it all fell apart when I was in high school. I'm still recovering. My parents' divorce turned my whole world upside down.

Your husband is not going to respond to your reinvention exactly the way you want him to, and you're going to freak out and think, "Holy shit, *he's* the problem! He doesn't know me or love me at all! If he's out of the picture, I'm going to be able to fix this!" That's normal and natural; we felt it ourselves, which is why we're comfortable talking to you "from the other side of things." What we can tell you is this: Don't hit the road if your husband is not fully on board with your reinvention. It takes time to make it happen, and it takes time for the results to show. It would be ideal to have him on board, of course, but just because he's not following along right away doesn't mean he never will.

> **Barb**
>
> Nobody should get a divorce during the first five years that you have kids. You literally wouldn't be happy with anybody. It's a huge adjustment period. How can anyone think clearly when you're in a state of chaos and adjustment?

Reinvent Your Family: Divorce Is Not an Option

At one time or another, like all women, we both have imagined a life without our husbands. We're not going to lie to you about that. We have both come to the realization, however, that divorce is NOT an option.

Barb

I had a huge fight with my husband because he was frustrating me. I was running around the house, making beds, in between doing things for work; he was sitting on the couch eating chips and salsa. I was enraged because this was not what I signed up for. I felt that our relationship was way out of balance. I felt trapped in my marriage. My husband was not responding to me, which led me to believe he didn't care. He was trapped, too—in a marriage that was short on intimacy with a woman who harped on him constantly. Not what he signed up for, either. I felt that every time we even had a productive talk, things would go right back to the old way again. I'd ask him to do something simple like change a lightbulb; he would say he'd do it, but it never got done. I was banging my head against the wall. I didn't know how things would ever get better. So one night we had this incredible fight, and he shouted at me: "I don't know why you married me in the first place!" Then I shouted back at him, "Well it's a little late for that now—we have kids!"

And that's when it hit me. I had an epiphany: How would I ever tell my kids that their dad wasn't living with us anymore? That day I decided to just take the idea of divorce off the table, and everything changed. My perspective cleared right up. In that moment I knew I was never going to get a divorce, that I loved my husband and my family.

When I realized we were in this for life, I realized it was pointless to fight every battle as it happened. We didn't have to focus on all the little things about one another that aggravated each of us. That's when I pulled myself out of the race and into the marathon. You've got to pace yourself much better in a marathon.

Now I just imagine getting a divorce, and I encourage women to try it. Instead of threatening to divorce my husband when he pisses me off, I have the divorce in my head but don't talk about it with him. It makes me feel that I'm not trapped—that I have options, even if they're only in my head, and that option always makes me want to stay.

RECONNECTING WITH YOUR PARTNER

Do you spend time alone with your husband now that you have kids? Do you find any time for romance? Do you think it will wait until the kids are grown? All of a sudden as couples we don't think we need to be a couple anymore. That we're just a family. So everything we do is as a family.

Says psychologist and life counselor Shelly Naphatal, "Even when you have little children, it's really important never to disconnect from your spouse. You can't put your relationship on hold for eighteen years and expect to say what are we going to do this morning out of the blue. That's a mistake. You have to stay connected and keep that way. Being intimate with your husband is really important to your relationship, and it's something you shouldn't really take for granted, even though we all do."

Barb

Part of getting my house in order meant getting my sex life back on track. I also found that if you have sex three times a week, you can pretty much get anything you want. I'm still working on that one.

"We forget that we actually need to create new couple history. Like a plant that thrives with water and sunlight, your marriage needs to be nurtured, too." Here are some things you should keep in mind, provided by clinical psychologist Dr. Michelle Golland:

- The biggest predictor of divorce is lack of humor. If even in the middle of an argument, there is some exchange of humor or laughter, you are probably not going down the divorce road.
- If you're not happy to see your husband when he comes home, you can bet he's not happy to see you. You need to change this around. Have five positive interactions with your spouse to every one negative and see how that changes things.
- As a couple you know each other's weakness. Do not go for the jugular.
- A couple should be going out minimally one time a month.

Children can put a lot of stress on a marriage, so make a date night, bring your sense of humor, and start creating new couple history.

TURN IT AROUND

When you change your perspective, you change your life. When you focus on the positive, on what works, instead of obsessing about what doesn't work, that changes everything. When you see petty annoyances for what they are, petty annoyances, you stop thinking "How can I escape this?" and turn your attention to "How do I make this work?"

Barb's "no-divorce option" changes everything. Once you decide that divorce is not an option, your perspective becomes completely different. You look more at the "big picture," that the power struggle can be turned into more productive teamwork. The constant power struggles lose their urgency. It's no longer a matter of what's pissing you off in the next five minutes; it's more about how you see the picture over the next fifty years. It's not about making your husband your nemesis; it's about seeing that you are in this together and how you're going to make it together. When your husband is your friend and your confidant, not your adversary or rival, you are actually able to get through things with greater ease and grace.

Jen

When Barb shared her "no divorce" epiphany, it definitely changed my perspective as well. When I looked at things that way, I could see that this husband of mine, this was the guy I married. He was the father of my children, and I really like and love him. This was the person I wanted to grow old with. When I was able to see that clearly—not these five seconds or five days, but five decades—I stopped overreacting to every little thing. I started giving more time and thought to how I was going to deal with things with him, because it mattered in the long term. I've gotten so much better at not going for the jugular. When you leave the door of divorce cracked open, you say meaner things. When you say and believe you're in it for life, you think about what those words mean for the long haul. If we're going to be together for another fifty years, we'd better make it a good fifty years! Simply: I knew I never wanted to get divorced. And now I had to live that way—as a person who didn't want to get divorced. More important, as a person who wants a loving, lifelong marriage.

You picked your husband for a reason, and you have to explore that reason to the fullest. You have to think about why you decided to try "forever" with him, and you have to remember that every day of your life. When you consider your happiness, consider all sides. You're not happy in a vacuum; your husband will be happier when he sees you happier. Everyone wins.

Give yourself some time. Give your husband time. None of this change happens immediately. The beauty of having a spouse, unlike having a boyfriend, is that you have the time—you have made a commitment for the rest of your lives, which means another

Jen

I'm still affected by my parents' divorce. I still have a hard time talking about it. I'm still profoundly sad about it, and I would never put my children through that.

twenty, forty, sixty years to work on things. Yes, you want to move along with your reinvention, but you have to pace yourself. It requires a lot of adjustment and commitment. Just like anything else in life, if you want to be successful, you have to do the work. If you don't do the work, there will be no fulfillment or success.

Reinvent Your Family: A Partnership Is a Two-Way Street

Sometimes you're going to bear the brunt of the load; sometimes your husband will. Having a partner at all is a benefit, even if you feel that the work is split 70/30.

MOTHER OF REINVENTION: MAHTAB

Family Business

MAHTAB HAKIM, thirty-eight, married eleven years, two kids (ages four and eight)

BEST ADVICE: *You have to have a passion for what you will be doing, to justify to yourself that you can take time away from your husband and children—and you need to be ready for that.*

"All my priorities have changed since becoming a mom. My family is my priority; I live and breathe them, and they factor into every decision I make. It has changed me drastically!

"I was a first-grade teacher for four years. I knew I wouldn't go back to teaching after I had a baby, because it would take all the time away from my child, and I couldn't justify it, especially when I was spending time with other people's children all day long. When Lola was born, I wasn't thinking about what I was going to do next. I was just enjoying her. Then, when she was about a year old and I stopped breast-feeding, I started getting the itch. I knew that if I did something, it had to be something that involved her, or I wouldn't do it. I knew I didn't want to work for anybody; I wanted to do something that was mine so that I could have my children with me.

"My husband told me to figure out what I wanted to do and he would support me 100 percent. I wanted to do something in retail, and first I thought it would be a women's clothing store. Then I thought accessories. Then one day Lola threw up all over her car seat. I went to the car wash, and they took out the car seat and I was stuck. I thought, 'What should I do? Where can I go to get this thing installed properly?' I was freaking out. That's when I realized that this was going to be my business. That I was going to open up a place that sells and installs car seats. My husband thought it was a brilliant idea. He told me do all the research, and I did—a full year of research every single day while my daughter napped and after she went to bed. At the end of that year I got certified and got my training. I knew everything I needed to open a store. My husband handled the entire financial aspect of it, and we took out a small business loan. I opened the store when Lola was 2½. She was with me every day until she went to school, and that is exactly how I wanted it.

"It has now been six years since we opened the store, and we have had success at it. I feel I have more respect for myself for doing it. I do feel empowered. I cannot wait to get up in the morning to come to work. I can't imagine doing anything but this; I love it! I feel revitalized. I love what I do. It is like a family here; it is wonderful.

"I thought working with my husband would create problems, but it has actually brought us closer together. You know we have this other thing in common besides our children and our marriage and just love for one another. We created this together you know, and I just love that part of our relationship, and it hasn't caused any friction. I think my husband loves seeing that I am passionate about something that is also benefiting both us and our family. Our children are at the age now where they see their mom has created this store and loves what she does, and it doesn't take time away from them, and it all works.

"You have to have it all well-thought out in your head so that you are happy doing what you are doing. You have to know what works for you and strive toward it. I know moms who are miserable working and not spending time with their children. Your career has to make sense in your life. Do something you love doing that brings joy into your life."

Mahtab proves that necessity is not the mother of invention; motherhood is the mother of invention! She found her reinvention from needing a good car seat, and now she has developed a whole business around it. Most important, she wanted to find a way to have a business in which she could still enjoy being with her children—and she did.

WHEN DIVORCE IS THE ONLY OPTION

We are both products of divorce. Analyzing our families, we know that there are times when divorce really is the only answer, and sometimes it's the answer that seems to work at the time. Barb is a product of the former. Her father was a substance abuser, and her parents divorced when she was young. It was essential to her health and her families' health that she not be a part of that world. Her mother made the decision to divorce because the marriage, especially considering the fate of young children, was the wrong situation for the family.

As we've said again and again, we're both married, each more than ten years, and we intend to stay that way. Our husbands may be annoying at times (and of course they find us annoying, too), but they are not a threat to us and our children or our overall sanity. But we do acknowledge that there are times when divorce is necessary—and in fact, sometimes a reinvention means just that.

In the following pages we address parenting outside a traditional context. Remember: We are both children of divorce, and we have some wisdom to impart from that front. But we've also talked to divorced mothers, widowed mothers, and other women who are parenting without traditional partners to bring you the advice that follows.

MOTHER OF REINVENTION: LINDA

Rebirth from Divorce

LINDA PERLMAN, forty-seven, divorced, one grown daughter and one seven-year-old daughter

BEST ADVICE: *It's never too late to bloom!*

"I have always shied away from anything that seemed too difficult or demanding. As a teen and young adult I found myself time and again going the safe route. I wouldn't dare raise my hand in class, and that became a metaphor for my life. I was a late bloomer, who "found myself" in middle age. I'm amazed now at my willingness to take on new adventures. It's an awakening that I thought might never come. What was I so scared of? Why did I worry so much? There's something about turning forty as a woman. It's the ultimate wake-up call; it's time to make things happen!

"I made a major change in my life a few years ago when I left a twenty-two-year marriage. Overall it was a happy marriage, but things had changed. I had changed. I said yes to a man I barely knew and spent more time picking out china for our registry and planning a big wedding than contemplating what marriage means.

"Deciding to get a divorce rocked every inch of my being. I crumpled up and then needed to be smoothed out again. It's been an amazing journey from my perceptive. I find myself now taking on tasks that would have been out of the question just a few years back.

"My oldest daughter went away to college this year. I insisted that she go out of town for school. I try not to play the blame game with my mother, but I was never encouraged to do the same, and in my efforts to improve on anything my mother did, I pushed my kid right out of the nest. When we moved her into the dorm, I had to stop myself from decorating it as my own. When she rushed her sorority, I felt every pain of her hell week. And when she gets homesick and cries and desperately begs to come home, I reassure her, but I don't give in.

"When I was thirteen I sat through many of my friends' bar and bat mitzvahs. I danced and celebrated with them. I also cringed at the thought of my being up there. Reading from the torah, speaking in front of others, and being in the spotlight was something that made me feel sick to my stomach. Now, at forty-seven, I will be a bat mitzvah this spring. After two years of classes and struggling to learn a new language, I will finally be a woman in the Jewish sense!

"After looking for a new house for the past two years, I decided I would find a property, knock down the house standing on it if need be, and darn it, build my own house—and that's exactly what I'm doing! When I meet with my architects, I sketch plans, give my ideas, and say an emphatic 'No!' when I don't like something. I truly surprise myself at times!

"Waking up every morning now, even when my alarm goes off before sunrise, I stretch and smile. I'm on the road to becoming the woman I always wished and hoped I could be."

Linda shows us that it is never too late to reinvent. She was a child, then an adult, who always played it safe. She dug deep to realize her reinvention, and now she is knocking down walls—literally and figuratively!

PARENTING WITH OTHER PARTNERS

If you are divorced, widowed, or just decided to go solo on parenting, there are other adults who come into play in your life as you navigate this decision. Whether your ex or a nanny or your mother, others will be affected by your reinvention and will also be there to support you. For now, let's look at reinvention in less traditional situations.

Plusses and Minuses

Stephanie Davis, divorced mother of two, shared her experience with us on our show. "Sometimes it's easier to be a single parent because you are General Mom. However, there's no fallback. When you're a single mom, you don't have to divide your time with a partner, so there's an enormous amount of intimacy and lack of distraction when you are with your children in terms of the quality of time."

There are pros and cons about navigating parenting and reinvention in a nontraditional family situation.

The big pro is that you don't really need anyone else's approval in your decisions. As the main caregiver to your children, your word is the final word. You also don't have to factor in someone else's needs and how they are going to affect your time with your children to the extent that you would have to if you had a full-time, equal partner. Yes, you have a relationship with your mother or sister or friend who is helping you juggle your parenting responsibilities with your reinvention, but the dynamic is completely different than it would be in trying to keep a marriage centered and straight.

But what is a plus in many ways is also a minus: On the downside, not having a "partner" in the classic sense means all the decisions really are yours and yours alone. That means a lot more of your brain space that could be allotted to focusing on your reinvention is being used up by basic daily tasks and considerations. Don't be discouraged!

You *can* do this. We know you can! In this section we give you pointers for dealing with your ex and some of the other adults who may be taking on a larger role in helping you raise your kids.

Navigating with an Ex

When there's been a separation or divorce, for the most part both parents continue to play a role in parenting. This is true if your kids are in preschool or if they are grown and have families of their own. How much or how little depends on the individual family, the terms of the split, the relationship of the exes, and sometimes just basic geography.

For the divorced ladies out there, good communication with your ex may not be a reasonable expectation. Miscommunication and a lack of understanding are probably among the reasons you got divorced in the first place! For this reason, it's okay to adopt the "on a need-to-know" basis. You may remain on friendly terms with your ex, which serves you well in working out matters having to do with your shared children. However, in terms of this person being your confidante, he may not be your most supportive choice. You should probably turn to one of your girlfriends— maybe one who's also a mom.

How is your reinvention going to affect your ex? Will you be less likely to be able to pick up the slack if he needs you to help out during his custody time? Are you going to be less available for things you may still do "as a family"? (Divorce or not, if you have kids with someone, that person is still part of the family.) Are you going to have less money to provide for the kids?

You don't need your ex's approval. Remember that the discussions can be opened on a "need-to-know" basis. If you want to take an art class as part of your reinvention and the time you choose to take it doesn't affect the normal flow of custody, does it warrant a discussion? On the other hand, if you're starting a new job and your time with your kids is going to be compromised because of it, then yes, you do need to have a talk with your ex. Will he take the kids later on Saturday so you can spend the morning with them? Would he consider taking them a couple of weeknights from time to time instead of on the weekend?

When you have these discussions with your ex, you must be very clear about what your priorities are, what your plan is, and how it is going to affect the time spent with your children.

You may be reading this and thinking: "You have no idea what an ass my ex is. I cannot sit down with him about something so personal. He will end up making me feel that I am a horrible mother and person, that I am selfish for even bringing this up." No matter how big an ass your ex is, remain firm and strong. Remember that what you're doing here is about you and also beyond you. Your wanting something for yourself is going to make you a better person and a better mother.

We're not saying it's going to be easy, but control what you can control. You cannot control his reaction, but you can control your decisions. Just be strong.

MOTHER OF REINVENTION: MARIE

A Fresh Start

MARIE, divorced, three kids

BEST ADVICE: *Change requires adjustment, but once you take that step, just know that with a little patience, faith, and perseverance, you will soon be moving forward on a stronger footing and accomplishing things you may never before have dreamed possible.*

"I had been married for half of my life. During that time there were many happy memories made, yet sadly, there were just as many difficult times. Unfortunately there comes a time when you know deep in your heart that you've tried everything you can. Although it still is not easy to face the fact that your marriage is falling apart—to imagine your children bouncing between two homes, splitting holidays, the awkwardness of sitting at the dinner table with one less person, taking separate vacations, attending sporting events and performances separately, and knowing you will now be a single parent in your community. In my mind I thought, this only happens to other people, not me. Then suddenly I knew that staying in a relationship just to avoid those things was not doing anyone any good and would end up hurting the children.

"That's when I realized I had to make a change in my life. This did not come easily, but it did give me a sense of relief when I started to believe in myself, and of course believe that the kids would benefit from a positive change in their lives, as well as watch their mom become a stronger, more independent role model in their lives, doing the best she can.

"I needed to go back to work after being home and raising my kids every day of their lives for the past seventeen years, and I knew finding a job was not going to be a simple task. I hadn't finished college and didn't have a degree to help myself compete with all the younger, freshly graduated, career-oriented individuals! But I didn't let that stop me from thinking positively and knowing that it would all work out.

"The year prior to this, I had taken a one-hour-a-day position at the local school, just for fun. I decided to inquire about any other positions within the school district or maybe another school in our area. Luckily, after just a few months of looking, I came upon a position that sounded perfect for me. It was an instructional aide at a local school. This was perfect for me because I absolutely love children and loved the thought of working with them! After just a short time I also began working one on one with various children who needed additional attention with reading skills. I have spent time with the reading specialists at the school, learning how to properly work with the children. I now have this desire to begin taking courses that will enhance what I am doing with these children. I leave work every day knowing I have made a difference in these little lives.

"In addition to taking on this new challenge for myself, I looked back and remembered how my mother had decided to go back to work when my brother and I were still in elementary school. I knew that we adjusted very well to that. We were good kids who made good choices and matured nicely because of our independence, which was created due to our mother's new working schedule. I felt confident that the same would take place in my home. Of course my kids are and always will be my priority, so if necessary, I would tend to their needs immediately to make the transition a smooth one for them.

"Fortunately, this newly acquired change in my life was received very well at home. All three of my children encouraged me to find a job when I told them I was thinking of going back to work. They were very supportive. Having their love and support made this change in my life even more fulfilling. That's when I knew we were heading in the right direction in this new chapter of our lives.

"It has been an eye-opening experience. Definitely an emotional one for me. But the strength I have gained from it has by far outweighed any pain endured from the start. Therefore, I can honestly say that I do not have any regrets and am still taking one day at a time with the newfound strength I never knew I had."

When Jen asked Dr. Wendy Mogel about the importance of being a role model for our children, Dr. Mogel replied that the most important thing is, "being a role model of enjoying being a parent, of pleasure in adult life." Marie was a great role model for her children. She showed them that you can't stay in a bad situation that will just end up harming everyone in the end, and that happiness can be found when you trust yourself and go after what you want.

REINVENTION AND YOUR CHILDREN

One of the biggest challenges you may have to overcome in setting your reinvention in motion is how it will affect your children and how they will respond to the changes happening, whether they're small, such as Mom's taking a walk for an hour every morning before school, or large, such as Mom's taking on a big job and may not be as available to us during the week as we're used to her being. So yes, your reinvention is about you, but as we've said, it affects everyone around you. The goal is to bring your family with you, not leave them behind. You want your children to view your reinvention as a positive thing.

Jen

My children had only known me as a stay-at-home mom. The only time I was away was for my much-needed workouts (an hour here or there) and the occasional date night with my husband (most nights I left right before or shortly after they went to bed). Because of my involvement with the parent association at their preschool, they were used to seeing me at school most days also. Since Barb and I were planning to work primarily during school hours, I did not anticipate my work affecting my kids at all. So much for the best-laid plans!

Lilah and Cooper didn't like the fact that instead of walking them in to school and lingering for awhile, I now just dropped them off (not a lot of time for hanging around). They were confused if I couldn't drive for a field trip or be a part of what goes on in school. I do not remember parents being around school as they are now. It seems that almost daily there are events at school needing parent participation. I have had to sit them down and have some discussions with them.

Whether you are dealing with small children or teenagers, your kids will notice the changes. They'll actually feel them happening. Children are more aware than we give them credit for, and small children especially are also much smarter than we sometimes realize. If our partners live by the mantra "happy wife, happy life," our kids live by it, too. Your children may not be able to grasp the complexity of why a reinvention is important for you and the health and happiness of the family, but at almost any age, they realize that if Mom's having a good day, everyone's having a good day—and it's just as true the other way around.

Reinvent Your Family:
Your Children Will Be Affected—In a Good Way

All that being said, the key to easing your children into a transition like this is to keep it as smooth and even as you possibly can. Because even though they can accept that you're happier and nicer to be around, if they're used to things being a certain way and one day you just pull the rug out from under them, no one's going to be happy.

A Family Affair

Once you have your husband on board, you need to hold a family meeting (if your kids are old enough to sit and listen) and talk about your reinvention. When you do, don't make it seem like a chore. Have a fun, upbeat attitude and explain to your children how you need them to help and how this reinvention is going to benefit them also. For your younger kids, emphasize how proud you are of them, that they're big enough to be a part of this kind of meeting. Always look for opportunities to focus on the positives.

Reinvent Your Family: Communication Is Key

Be enthusiastic. Don't lecture them on how they're going to have to "start pulling their weight around here." Instead, approach the situation as a positive, happy person who has discovered something wonderful that will benefit everyone else—that will enrich and improve everyone else's life! Once you have them all jazzed up that this is going to be a thrill for everyone, then get into how everyone's going to have to get together to bring the reinvention to fruition. Don't be apologetic that everyone will have a role to play; be thrilled that you can include everyone in this wonderful endeavor.

Here's something that you need to think about before opening your mouth to your family: Communication is a two-way street. Strong communication with your family is going to make a huge difference in how smoothly all of this will go. We can tell you from our own experience with this, and all the unnecessary anger, frustration, and fighting that went on without strong communication, that you'll get much better results with honey than you will with vinegar.

Barb

Here's how I presented what I was planning with Jen to my husband and kids: "Guys, I'm going to be doing this really fun thing with Jen! And while we're working, you can play with her kids!" Even just the enthusiasm that I brought to the idea helped very much.

In addition to you telling them what you need from them, you need to listen to how they think and feel about everything—both your husband and your kids. The more your family feels they can have a voice, the more willing they're going to be to help you. You're also going to have to take their comments and concerns under real consideration as you continue navigating your way through reinvention. Just because you're staking your claim and making a declaration doesn't mean you get exactly what you want. Listen to them and hear them. Don't be so stuck in your own situation that you don't realize there will be repercussions.

Most important, with your spouse or your family, don't just wing it. Come with a plan. Be as specific as possible about what you're planning, how you came to this decision, and in which ways everyone will need to pitch in. Say something like this: "I've been doing a little exploring, and here's what I'm going to do. I have a plan for how we can do this together, and I'm excited to share it with you."

When talking to your kids, be very clear about what the changes are going to be. If you're going to spend fewer hours during the day with them, let them know that. But also make sure that when you're with them, you're focused on them. If they feel that when you're with them you're really there, that will go a long way to helping them accept what's happening.

If the changes you're going to be making mean spending less time with your family, shifting responsibilities, or otherwise shuffling the status quo, you really don't want to "hit and run." Sit down and talk with them. Let them know gradually how things are going to change. Reassure them that the changes are positive and give them real examples they can comprehend about why these changes are so good for everyone. For younger children, tell them something along the lines of this: "I have great news. Every Tuesday Grandma is going to pick you up from school. She's really excited about spending more time with you. She's been wanting to have a 'special time' with you—and to have you all to herself. Won't that be great!" For older kids, try something like this: "My going back to work means more family trips or getting the sneakers you want." Keep it positive.

Also be sure that when you're with the children, you're truly present. When they feel that you are with them, the good feelings will go a long way toward gaining their cooperation.

Reinvent Your Family: Keep Children Actively Involved

When we started all this, we shared a babysitter. Sometimes there was no babysitter. Sometimes we just talked and dreamed and built ideas while we watched our kids play. We planned road trips. We'd take a long drive to a kid-friendly place like LegoLand and talk in the car. We found the time. Get creative. This is definitely something we've mastered over the years that we've been working together! We show our kids everything about the show. We include our kids in lots of the fun aspects of our show. We have even brought them into editing.

Barb

I feel that because my reinvention has given me something else to focus on, I'm not so focused on my husband or my kids, which makes me a better wife and mother. Your kids don't need all that focus on them, and your husband doesn't need all that attention, either. It's okay to swing the pendulum back in your direction.

Include your kids in any way you can. If you're going to open a cupcake shop, tell the kids that they're the taste testers. We've also somehow managed to master getting our kids involved. It's not like we're going to drag them into our work, but when we film our shows, crews come over and the kids are around. They find it all very exciting, especially when we can find a way to bring them in on the action. When Soraya was five years old, she even filmed some reality footage for one of our episodes. She was very proud.

ARE YOU A HELICOPTER PARENT?

When we sat down with Dr. Wendy Mogel, author of *Blessing of a Skinned Knee* and *Blessing of a B-Minus*, we saw that some of the things we think we're supposed to do as good mothers are the exact things that eat up most of our time—and also kill our kids' self-confidence. If you want your kids to be empowered, you have to help them get that way. Here's Wendy's advice: "Pretend you have six children. Because if you had six children you couldn't be wiping all their butts and cushioning all their falls. It's important to broaden the definition of an emergency. An emergency is not if a child is in a slightly bad mood or is a little bit hungry," meaning it's actually important to let your children experience those things and work through them themselves. As she explains,

It's how they develop the muscle to tolerate all the challenges of life. The media loves to feed parents rare but highly sensational events to terrify us to the point that we watch over our kids constantly. Then we send them to college. We need to let them be exposed to all kinds of dangers while they're younger so they can practice using good judgment now, while the stakes are very low. You have to let your child fall sometimes. It allows them to learn from the experience. Our job is to raise our children to be able to leave us, and in order for them to do that, they need to develop their own skills to cope and survive.

The best gift you can give your child is to teach him or her to be independent; in doing so, you'll be giving yourself a gift as well: more time to focus on, nurture, and care for you. You may have to clean up a few messes and tend to a few scraped knees, but the confidence your child will gain will be well worth it. And what you will be able to achieve for yourself and your own reinvention is the icing on the cake.

Everyone Pitches In

Dr. Wendy Mogel
"We are treating our kids like handicapped royalty. This is what I call 'good parents gone bad.' Loving, devoted, intelligent parents who act like kids can't even wipe their own butts or walk down the street three houses until they're thirty-five."

One way of looking at having your kids help out around the house is that it helps give you more free time to think about what you want to be doing. But it really isn't just a matter of lightening the load. When kids have responsibilities, when they can contribute to the family, it actually empowers them. Sure, they may fight you at first about having to set the table, or get the mail, or feed the dog, but when they get into it and see how they're helping you, it actually makes them feel more important. They have a purpose and a function in the family; the efforts they make really matter to how the family and the household run.

Getting back to the expectations we impose on ourselves, a large part of what we do to ourselves is that we feel guilty if we don't do everything. Crazy, but it happens all the time. It happens sometimes without us realizing it. We go about our routines, doing everything for everyone, and it doesn't really occur to us that we can hand over that dust rag, and that that will be a positive thing. We think we have to do everything, and as a result we also deprive our kids of something that can be really great for them—building skills and self-confidence by helping out.

Reinvent Your Family:
Help Your Kids by Letting Them Help You

Of course you're not going to try to get your three-year-old to vacuum or your six-year-old to make dinner, but there are a ton of age-appropriate tasks children can accomplish as soon as they begin to really comprehend language. Your two-year-old can pick up blocks and put them back in a box. Your six-year-old can unload the dishwasher—even if he just stacks the dishes on the countertop and doesn't actually put them away. Your eight-year-old can set and clear the table. Your ten-year-old can sort the laundry, and your twelve-year-old can fold it. Your teenagers can walk the dog or change the litter box; they can do their own laundry and even be responsible for making simple weeknight dinners.

It is also important to encourage your children to play on their own. It frees up time for you, but also teaches your children a valuable lesson about being independent.

WHAT CAN YOUR KIDS DO?

It may surprise you!

AGE	TASKS
2–3	• Put away toys
	• Put dirty clothes in the hamper
	• Stack books and magazines
	• Fill the pet dish (with a little help)
	• Wipe up spills
	• Lightly dust
4–5	*All of the above, plus:*
	• Make their own beds
	• Empty wastebaskets
	• Clear the table
	• Water plants
	• Fix a bowl of cereal
6–7	*All of the above, plus:*
	• Sort laundry
	• Sweep floors
	• Help make and pack lunch
	• Set the table
	• Straighten up the bedroom
	• Pour drinks
	• Answer the phone

8–9   *All of the above, plus:*
- Load the dishwasher
- Put away groceries
- Help make dinner
- Put away own laundry
- Peel vegetables
- Make toast
- Walk the dog

10–12   *All of the above, plus:*
- Unload the dishwasher and put dishes away
- Fold laundry
- Clean the bathroom
- Cook simple meals
- Do laundry
- Mow the lawn
- Make and change own bed
- Clean the kitchen
- Babysit younger siblings *(with adult in the home)*

Source: WebMD.com, About.com

Important note: Don't make this a "you have to do this" situation. Remember that part of this is about empowerment. Tell your kids what needs to be done, and let them know how confident you are that they can really get the task done. When they feel that they're really pitching in, it is kind of amazing to watch kids do their jobs. They really rise to the occasion. Being children, they may give you a hard time at first, and they may not always be enthusiastic about what they have to do. Even then, be consistent. They need to follow through even if they don't want to. If they have been given a task, it is theirs to do; if they don't complete it, there must be clear consequences for their inaction.

Another important note: Do not *ask* your kids to do the things you want them to do. Tell them what their responsibilities are. You don't have to come off as a drill sergeant, but at the end of the day, you're the boss. **Remember, they are helping you get more "you" time; you are helping them prepare for life.** How will they know how to fend for themselves if you do every little thing for them? When you think about it that way, really, it's a win-win situation.

Jen

We have a chore chart on our kitchen wall that includes what is expected of our kids daily. It lists each day and each task the kids are expected to accomplish that day. It has been very helpful in guiding them and not having to remind them. They can go to the chart and see what they have to do. I'm not saying it's a perfect science, but it definitely gets the ball rolling.

Be One Thing at a Time

One of the most important things you need to do if you are not able to spend the amount of time you used to with your children is that when you are with them, really BE with them. Do not have your Blackberry in one hand while attempting to focus on your kids. UNPLUG! Yes, of course it's hard in this day and age, when there is always something that you need to check, but you have to compartmentalize. This is one of our biggest challenges as well.

Try to set clear work hours for yourself, so when you're with your kids, you are *with your kids*. Give them your attention. They notice; don't think they don't. They need you and your undivided attention. Get to know them, what they like, who they are. Spend time with them doing something that is important to or fun for them, even if it doesn't really interest you. Give them you. They want and need you, whether they are five or fifteen. The teenagers may be pushing you away, but they need you, too. Quality of time is more important than quantity of time. This is not to say that you should be absent and then swoop in for a half hour, but just be there for them.

Of course there are going to be times when you absolutely have to take a phone call, or you're on an impossible deadline, or you can't help but split your time between your children and the rest of your life, but as much as you can, try to create clear boundaries and abide by them.

MOTHER OF REINVENTION: LAUREN

Embracing the Unexpected

LAUREN BOOTH, forty-one, married thirteen years, four kids (ages twelve, ten, six, and four)

BEST ADVICE: *If something is working, do more of that. Figure out what gives you joy and find ways to make small and consistent efforts to do those things.*

"I have always been a creative and visual person. I get a lot of peace and joy from the creative process. Maybe experiencing the ultimate creative process, that of making a baby—four of them—opened something else in me.

"I had my first reinvention at twenty-four. I had known the man who would later become the father of my children for a total of about three weeks when I had a yard sale, sold my car, and bought a one-way ticket out of Los Angeles and the single life. We married and moved to London.

"In 1998 our first little guy was born. I was afraid when I was pregnant that my husband and I would never have any time alone again. I went on a three-week silent meditation retreat just before giving birth. I was sure I was going to have postpartum depression; I was a little, maybe hormonally, focused on the negatives of pregnancy. When Miles popped out, I was completely surprised by the wonder and love of it all. My world just got bigger; I like the noise.

"In 2000 our second little one came along. I think she was about eight months old when I got my first studio outside the home. I'll never forget walking home the first day from my studio and feeling guilty that I was making a conscious decision to leave my sweet baby and toddler. Was this the way that a really good mom behaved? My mom quickly popped into my head. She is a wonderful mom and friend, and I am very lucky, grateful, and humbled to have her as my role model for parenting. My mom always worked. I realized that I respected my mom for working and that it didn't detract from her being there 100 percent for me. This gave me confidence that maybe I could also combine being a good mom and still pursue something for myself.

"I was really interested in learning how to make things better, so I took a two-year sculpture course at Kensington Chelsea College in London, where I had a great teacher. I also got a studio in Notting Hill near to my kids' schools. I spent on average twenty hours a week there for the past eight years making sculpture, and other art, and sometimes doing nothing.

"We recently sold our home in London and moved to Connecticut, where we knew not a soul. I am in the process of finishing a new studio, so it's a clean slate once again. Our kids are doing well in their new schools, they are getting a little older, and I am curious where this next stage in life will take me. This has been my most recent change.

"When I arrive in my studio I turn off the phone and lock the door. It's my oasis. Mark is very supportive and encouraging of my art. I don't think we ever had a timeline or specific talk about my getting a studio or having a show. We all know the saying, 'happy wife, happy life.'

"I am very fortunate to have a really supportive partner. My husband has Parkinson's disease and has had it for ten years now. One, if not the most, difficult part of this disease for him is the restrictions it puts on his ability to do certain things with our kids. In some ways he's there for them more as a result of his illness; he works from home, and they see him daily dealing with challenging physical situations with dignity, calm, and presence. But it can be very difficult. I think we work well together as a team. I think we both expect each other to do the best we can, to communicate, be kind, and have fun together.

"I think many women wrestle with the feeling that we are doing a lot of things and maybe none of them particularly well. I definitely feel that way sometimes, but I also feel very fulfilled. I feel grateful all the time. Mark sometimes says that despite the suffering that comes with his disease, he wouldn't give it up because that is part of the whole package of our life, and if he gave that up, what else would not have happened and be happening in our lives? I feel that way about decisions in the past. I do continue to strive to do more, grow, be calm, and enjoy every moment. I have career goals that I have not yet met, but then I never thought I would have four children, either, and I don't think there is any level of career success that could have ever given me the fulfillment that being a mom does.

"Being a parent and wife cuts to the core of my Self. My children bring out every emotion in me, good and bad, and some I would like to think I didn't possess. Sometimes I feel that everything's in harmony. But right then I get thrown again. I think my work helps me to enjoy my children more.

"Maybe the first step of reinventing oneself is being happy with who you are. My mom's goal for my brother and myself was to raise happy, independent kids. I hope the choices I make, while not only working for my peace of mind, also help me to be a better mom. I just always try to do what feels right. I hope it's working for the kids."

Wow. Lauren is incredible! Did you notice that most of the women we interviewed talked about "happy wife, happy life"? A coincidence? We think not. The other thing about Lauren is that she's living proof of "no excuses." Obstacles get in your way, and they always will. If you want to reinvent badly enough, you will find your way around, over, or even through them.

Managing Your Expectations of Them

Also, don't fall into the trap of overscheduling your kids. Just like us, kids need downtime. They need to be able to have pockets of time when they can just think, dream, and imagine. Our expectations of ourselves aren't the only unfair ones we hold. When we impose our "hyper-expectations" on our kids, they actually don't thrive. As Dr. Wendy Mogel explains, "Deans call the incoming students coming into college 'tea cups' and 'crispies.' The tea cups are the ones who have been overprotected, and the crispies are the ones who are all burned out from too much over-scheduling."

This kind of constant shuffling around of kids actually affects them far more than your not being around as much.

If you notice that your kids are acting out, their grades are suffering, or their mood isn't what it used to be, talk to them. Talk to their teachers, friends, and anyone who can give you insight into what is going on with them. Seek outside help if necessary. You have made the decision that your family is always your number one priority. We do not get this time back, so as important as your reinvention is, it should never come at the expense of your family's well-being.

Your children may not be all that interested in why you need to make these changes in your life, but there are important things you can convey with your words and actions that will help them have at least some sense of appreciation for what you are doing (even if the "why" isn't exactly clear), and when they understand that there are benefits for everyone.

Betsy Brown Braun, parenting expert and author

"One of the things that I think gets overlooked is that when families have rituals together, they're working as a team. They operate together, and it creates a sense of belonging, and unfortunately what we do is say, 'I want her to be on the soccer team' or 'I want them to be on the baseball team,' but we forget about the family team. Think about when you're having dinner together with the family or if you always do something one way. The kids know what they're going to get, and what they're going to get is you."

Boundaries Make Happy Families

It's important for your children to see you happy and enjoying your adult life, and also important for them to understand that no matter what you're up to, they are always your priority. It's important for them to have a sense of purpose in their own lives and the confidence and skills to become more and more self-sufficient. Finally, it's important to have boundaries—and to adhere to them. For example, if you work from home, there has to be a clear definition of when you are unavailable to them and when you will be available again, and an understanding that they are not to barge in on you during "your time." Educate your children and husband about taking time for yourself; make that understanding like gospel and be sure to keep firm. If you flip-flop, all you're going to create is frustration and confusion.

EXCERPTED FROM "THE INVISIBLE WOMAN"

One night, a group of us were having dinner, celebrating the return of a friend from England. Janice had just gotten back from a fabulous trip, and she was going on and on about the hotel she stayed in. I was sitting there, looking around at the others all put together so well. It was hard not to compare and feel sorry for myself as I looked down at my out-of-style dress; it was the only thing I could find that was clean. My unwashed hair was pulled up in a banana clip and I was afraid I could actually smell peanut butter in it. I was feeling pretty pathetic, when Janice turned to me with a beautifully wrapped package, and said, "I brought you this." It was a book on the great cathedrals of Europe. I wasn't exactly sure why she'd given it to me until I read her inscription: "To Charlotte, with admiration for the greatness of what you are building when no one sees."

In the days ahead I would read—no, devour—the book. And I would discover what would become for me, four life-changing truths, after which I could pattern my work: No one can say who built the great cathedrals—we have no record of their names. These builders gave their whole lives for a work they would never see finished. They made great sacrifices and expected no credit. The passion of their building was fueled by their faith that the eyes of God saw everything.

NOW YOU KNOW

Reinvention takes work, and it also takes some cooperation from your family. In this chapter, we learned that:

- Everything is *not* your responsibility. Things will get done, eventually, even if not on your terms or your schedule.
- Your role of "default parent" also makes you the "general" of your family. If you're making it all work every day, you can restrategize to make it work for *you*.
- Reinvention affects everyone in your family, and positively, but as changes are happening, your family won't always see it that way.
- Your husband needs your attention and love.
- Your kids are capable of more than you realize.

Chapter 4

Reinvent Your Village
What's in Your Backyard?

I definitely felt, when I was at home with my twins, that there was nobody out there for me. I had no role model I could relate to. June Cleaver was the 1950s. Who were the real moms dealing with the same things I was dealing with these days? All the high-profile media moms like Angelina Jolie or Kelly Ripa weren't quite existing in the same world as us. Who was the person mothers like me could aspire to be? Who was there to guide us?

I felt it would have been so great if there was a show out there that addressed what we real moms were going through. But who was going to create it? At first, we didn't realize it was going to be us!

—*Barb*

As we planned our reinventions, we had very specific parameters that we both felt happy and comfortable working within. We both knew we wanted to be available for school drop-offs and pickups. We wanted to do something that wouldn't monopolize all our time—something that would allow us to spend plenty of quality time with our families. We also had a dollar amount for how much money we wanted to make, and we wanted to do something around a topic we were passionate about: motherhood.

At this stage in our lives, we were consumed and obsessed by motherhood, and it's all we talked about. We'd talk all the time about what was working in our families and what wasn't. We were each other's sounding boards, and that is what led us to decide what we wanted to do: namely, create a show like *The View*, but specifically for moms.

We wanted it to be simple, to talk about the things we always talked about; the real conversation moms were having. We always had questions and wanted a forum to collect and share answers. We had no idea at first that we were actually going to host it. (Even Jen, the casting director, never saw herself cast in it.) But that's how it all came together. It's all been very organic, very natural.

We're not celebrities or actors. Neither of us had ever produced a TV show before, so we decided to work on a smaller scale. We knew a lot of people were creating their own shows via the Internet, and that's what we decided we could accomplish within our parameters.

We understood that if the show really took off, it would take us away from our families and defeat what we were trying to do in the first place, so we brought it down in scope. We made it realistic and made it fit our needs.

We didn't do it alone. Discover how you, too, can pull it all together with your own village.

So you've gotten this far in the book, and you should now be committed to your reinvention, have explored the ways to carve out the time, have started thinking about what your passions are and what direction you're headed in, and have discussed this with your family and/or any caretakers in your life. Now is the time to broaden your approach and see exactly what and who you have access to. You may be surprised by the gems that lie right in your own backyard.

GET OUT OF YOUR OWN WAY

Like everyone else working toward a goal, we faced obstacles. We still had small children who were limited in what they could do for themselves. We still had limits on how much time we could devote to our reinvention. We didn't want someone else to drop off and pick up our kids at school. And of course we were already worn thin by the responsibilities and obligations we already had in our lives. But we also knew that we didn't want to miss out on the opportunity to reach our full potential as women.

This is going to happen with you as well. You're going to come up with a bunch of excuses why you can't make your reinvention happen. Some of these reasons may seem more important than others, and some may very well be. Don't neglect to evaluate them and look for ways that you *can* do what you want. Now is the time to let go of the excuses and look for the solutions.

You probably already know some of the things that are carrying more weight than necessary. Here's an example: an unfolded load of laundry versus a twenty-minute hike. Where are you going to find the most joy in those twenty minutes? The laundry will be waiting for you in the morning, and if you take twenty minutes of "me time" to take that hike, you'll be more energized to face the laundry, either later tonight or early tomorrow. No one's going to die if you don't do the laundry, but you will be a hell of a lot more cranky if you don't take that hike.

Reinvent Your Village:
Keep Your Eye on the Big Picture

The point is that we encountered plenty of obstacles. Some were inevitable; some we placed there ourselves. We did, and so will you. But you can't let these obstacles divert you from your reinvention. You have to continually keep your eye on the big picture and try not to get too tripped up over the little bumps. A big fight with your husband may make you want to throw in the towel, but don't. This is as important to you as getting up in the morning—and it will make getting up in the morning that much more fun!

So yes, you are going to be able to find a million reasons why you have no time to do this. And what you're going to have to do is to make a conscious decision about how badly you want this, then follow through. We can give you the tools and take you through our journey, but you have to want this reinvention if you're going to get it for yourself.

Things are going to crop up and get in your way every moment of every day. Maybe your mom calls, and you stay on the phone too long. Maybe your babysitter's sick or just doesn't show up one day. Maybe you have an inevitable errand to run or one of your kids gets sick. That's life. You still have to keep going. You have to face down everything that's going to pop up in front of you and keep your eyes on the prize. It's easy to get sidetracked from something you're doing for yourself to deal with the things you have to do for others. Just make it a point to get back on track as quickly as possible.

HONE IN ON YOUR PASSION

Each of our passions came from our own experience in mother-hood. We knew how we were feeling: overwhelmed and di-sheveled, crazed and alone. Were other moms as put together as they seemed? Were other women with children not having sex with their husbands? In finding each other and talking it out with each other, we realized that there were many more women out there feeling just as we were.

We wanted to connect to them and let them feel they had a "place" where they, too, could come and share their feelings with other moms. We knew moms don't have a lot of time to reach out. On top of that, we wanted to give them realistic advice and information they could really use—and give it to them in small "bites" so they wouldn't have to commit a half hour or more that they didn't have and could also watch on their own time. We wanted women to feel they were not alone, and through a web show we hoped to accomplish that.

We also saw a void in the market: No one was doing a show that was just for moms. No one was having a real conversation that included reality footage from their own lives. The goal was to create a forum for women to share and not feel alone. It was an idea that was very close to our hearts, and we were excited to get into it. It was also something we could rely on ourselves and our own resources to accomplish, which is very important to reinvention.

SET THE REINVENTION IN MOTION

We didn't wake up one morning and say, "We really need to do a show on the Internet!" In fact, when we started this, we didn't know very much about online programming. Jen's brother was doing some online programming, but we ourselves had not really tuned in to that world yet. But because it made sense for us on so many levels, it was an avenue worth exploring. It was something we could do on a reasonable scale, as far as time and financing were concerned. And it was something we could do from either of our living rooms.

We knew we were onto something, and scheduled as much time together as we possibly could to get our ideas out there and start to flesh them out into our actual show. We got together and got our kids to play together while we brainstormed. We had staked our claim on our reinvention, and we were moving full steam ahead.

That doesn't mean all was right in our worlds. Our children did their part by playing nicely while we worked, but our husbands didn't quite take us seriously—at least in the beginning. We had a show to create, and neither of us had ever done anything quite like this before.

We needed help. We needed to call upon people in our circle to help us with the information and tools we lacked. And when we exhausted that circle, we had to broaden it.

MOTHER OF REINVENTION: ANNE (PART 2)

Keeping "New"

ANNE TRACY EMERSON, forty, married for sixteen years, two kids (ages ten and five)

BEST ADVICE: *You can't throw money or stuff at kids to make them happy. They want your praise and attention. If you can give them that and still save a little for yourself, then you are doing all right.*

"I was an Emmy award–winning network producer when I had my son. Afterward, I hired a full-time nanny and took a writing job with a little field producing thrown in. It sounded good, but it was not ideal. I worked from dawn till way after dusk, still traveling whenever requested, and I saw my infant son only when the nanny brought him by the studio for a quick cuddle. When I called my brother one day whining about my life, he said, "If you are happy letting the nanny raise your child then so be it. Just be sure you understand that's exactly what's happening right now." I was shocked. I had no intention of letting someone else 'raise' my child.

"My husband and I decided to leave LA and move to a place where we could get by on less, but I would still have to work. After I had my second child, I decided to try to muddle my way through the freelance writing and producing world, but I found my real calling with a couple of the other mothers at the playground.

"I AM LOVE: Kids' Yoga Journey was the very first yoga iPad application just for kids. It was immediately named one of the 'hot' apps by iTunes and will soon be crossing over into the Android market.

"I love the challenge of using all of my writing and communicating skills to build the brand of Kids' Yoga Journey. We take videos of new poses and yoga classes at local schools. I am constantly posting photos and stories or just a little inspiration. Not only are we actively writing new stories, we are building a great fan base and support network with mommy bloggers, yogi bloggers, and children advocacy organizations who also believe that there is a healthy and fun way to use technology.

"Since I started investing more heavily in Kids' Yoga Journey as my main business, my family loves it. I am happy at home so much more than ever before. I've always relied heavily on sitters and nannies, and now if our team has children around during a Kids' Yoga Journey meeting, we see it as a bonus: We can test new poses on them. The team's children are some of the children in our Kids' Yoga Journey series.

"Having said that, I think whoever mentioned to me that you had more time to do your own thing when your children are a little older (five and ten) was dead wrong. Your life is carpooling them all over town! Now I work from 8:00 a.m. until 2:00 p.m. and then pretty much give up until they go to sleep.

"I would never have been able to make this transition to writing interactive stories for children on mobile apps if I had not stayed relevant in my field. I kept a hand in technology and my own interests all along. I also think it is important to really talk to and learn from people younger than yourself. I am a huge fan of the twenty-year-olds. My babysitters know that I will be peppering them with questions about what technology they use and why. I also make it a habit to read about the latest trends in fields that interest me, and that runs a really wide track. You never know how a bike rental business in Paris may actually relate to your own business model one day."

Ann literally found her inspiration in her backyard, connecting with other moms on the playground. She took casual conversation with other women watching their kids play and saw the potential of what they could all bring to the table. The point is, you should always keep your eyes and ears open. You never know when, or with whom, inspiration might strike.

TAKE THE NEXT STEP

Now our idea was in place: a five-minute web show geared toward moms. It was time to make that idea into a reality. How do you do that? You start by looking in your backyard!

Because we were planning to do a show, we needed to put together a "sizzle reel," which is essentially a three-minute collage of us and moments from our show (which at the moment only existed in our heads and hearts). For that we needed money. The problem was that no one would put up the money we needed—not until we had that sizzle reel, or a sample of the show. So we had to put in our own money. We talked to our husbands about what we could each comfortably contribute and came up with five thousand dollars each (and that wasn't a pretty conversation with either of our husbands!). That wasn't much for what we needed to accomplish, so we were definitely going to have to get creative, which included asking for favors.

We had a company interested in our idea, and they said they needed us to deliver the sizzle reel in two weeks! We had no idea at the time what a sizzle reel was and had limited funds. (The good news is that the company supplemented our original budget, but we were still working on a "skeleton" budget.) We looked at each other, not having much of an idea what to do; rolled up our sleeves; and started figuring out who we knew, what they knew, and how they could help us.

At first the idea of asking favors and calling on people we didn't know very well seemed daunting, but we knew that to make this a reality, we were going to have to put ourselves out there. Jen called a mom from her school who she knew used to be a director. At the time she didn't know her well. As luck would have it, this mother of three young boys was also getting the itch to do something outside of the family and jumped on board. An additional bonus is that now she is a dear friend to both of us—what a wonderful by-product!

Barb called on a friend of her husband's who had a production company to help out with the day-to-day production of putting the reel together. Next, Jen called on two other mom friends she had, one a psychologist and the other an author. They both agreed to be "guests" on this makeshift show.

We called on a mutual friend we met in our Mommy & Me class who is a stylist, and she also agreed to help out. Our stylist friend also hooked us up with an amazing makeup artist, whom we use to this day. Barb also convinced one of her college friends to make an appearance. We moved Jen's living room around to look like a set, bought clothes (Okay, we tucked in the tags and returned everything afterward. . . . We did not have that in the budget!), and jumped into our first shoot day.

We developed the ideas based on conversations we had had during our years of hanging out with our kids and from all the conversations we were having with other moms. We wanted to share our lives, so we started going through all our home video footage to include real-life moments to support the topics we were talking about with our guests. We did this on a very limited budget and while making no money.

When we completed the finished sizzle reel and watched it, we felt exhilarated. We all knew we were onto something.

MOTHER OF REINVENTION: CANDICE (PART 2)

Marketing Maven to Community Activist

CANDICE PATE, thirty-six, married seven years, two kids (ages three and five)

BEST ADVICE: *Have faith that the reinvention will work itself out. It's a process.*

"I had always thought I would be a working mom. I am very type A, achievement oriented, and previously had derived a lot of my self-worth from my job. I was able to transition out of my old job with a generous severance package and breezed into full-time mother-hood with the peace of mind that I had taken advantage of an opportunity I simply couldn't pass up. Lo and behold, I loved it! I spent time with my baby and soon enough was pregnant with my second, and before I knew it I was a stay-at-home mom to two little ones.

"When my youngest was about three, I started to feel a little bored. Though I loved spending time with the kids, I had settled into a status quo in which life was pretty easy, with no real lows, but no highs, either. I missed some of the exhilaration of a big win at work, and I was tired of not having something more to define who I was at cocktail parties, so to speak.

"I needed a change, but wasn't sure how or what to do about it. I really didn't feel I could go back to the corporate world, but had no idea what else I could do. So I think I just put it off and fig-ured changing locations would take up a lot of time and energy.

"We moved, and I dove into life in our new town, and even ran the kid's school fund-raiser. I explored starting a ceramics business, partnering with a local potter, but that just fizzled. Even as I tried to commit to getting something off the ground, I eventually just lost steam. It felt really defeating, and I blamed myself for not wanting it badly enough, not working at it. Had I become lazy? Now that I have some distance, I can see it just wasn't the right thing.

"Time went by. Now I was really bored, and then in July, the Economic Development Board (EDC) called; they had a vacancy and were looking for someone with a marketing background. Was I still interested? I met with them and was appointed. I then began interfacing with the people doing the strategic marketing efforts for the city. I volunteered hundreds of hours and was finally hired as the interim CMO to lead the development of a strategic marketing plan for Sun Valley. I presented the plan to the city, and it was a huge hit.

"Putting it out there is definitely the first step in getting the ball rolling. Try not to get down on yourself because it's a really hard process, and the negativity will only prolong the agony. Stay positive, relish the place where you are in life while still pursuing your next chapter. I didn't believe, and that contributed to a lot of self-doubt, which was harmful to both myself and the process of trying to get back into the workforce. Even if this job doesn't pan out, I know I can do it. I feel as though a new chapter in my life has begun."

Notice that Candice, after taking several years to be home with her family, used skills she had gained from being a stay-at-home mom to get back into the workforce. Many of us are so busy going through the motions of our daily lives, we don't realize that most of the things we're juggling can actually be quite relevant outside the home!

ENJOY THE SMALL SUCCESSES!

At the last minute, we learned our sizzle reel was going to be included in a big presentation in New York, and we needed to go there to be interviewed on stage.

Jen

This was a big deal. I had gone from five years of not working, to having this idea for a web show, to going to New York and presenting it. We knew we were onto something, something that could be big.

We felt like such nobodies at this huge event, and we were overwhelmed at first. We were almost the last to present, and that gave us time to take in what we were seeing and plan how we would handle ourselves up there, on stage, in front of a thousand people.

Barb

The theater was so cold, I started shaking and freaking out. Jen pulled me into the bathroom, which was the warmest spot, and started giving me advice (thank goodness Jen used to be a casting director). Jen told me to make sure to repeat the question that the host, Billy Bush, asked and to look over the audience to the back of the house if people's stares were freaking me out. She assured me that she had my back even though I felt like vomiting.

Our sizzle reel played, and then we were interviewed by Billy Bush, who said to us, "What a great idea. I can't believe my wife didn't think of this!" Later we overheard him saying to someone else about us, "This is gonna be the show that will get sold."

Then we went back home, back to reality, and we waited for word. We were so exhilarated and alive. We couldn't believe that this idea that we thought up while playing with our kids was resonating with others, and we even got a free trip to New York out of it.

MOTHER OF REINVENTION: DIANA

Joining the Work Force at Sixty

DIANA LEVITT, sixty, getting a divorce after thirty-eight years of marriage, five kids

"I always knew I wanted children. I was twenty-five when I had my first and nearly forty-two when I had my fifth! I am supremely proud of the young people they have become, and they are my greatest achievement.

"I left school at eighteen, worked in the fashion industry in London for awhile, and at just twenty went to Spain. A year later I went home, and my real life began. I was offered the job of running a small manufacturing clothing boutique, which employed my ability for getting things done and managing people. Little did I know how these abilities would help me later in life raising a family and moving everyone across the pond!

"I got married the next year and had my first child two years later. In the society I lived in in London, women did not work after having children, and so it was for me. I never regret that I was a stay-at-home mother and will be eternally grateful that I was able to do so. I never missed working, but I always shared in world events and my husband's business by talking to him at the end of every day. I had asked him not to let me become a cabbage after not going out into the working world myself. My job was to run the household, his was to bring in the money, and our shared job was to raise our family.

"After my husband left initially, in 2002, I spent years feeling terrified and lonely. He came back twice after that, and he left for the last time in May 2009. I knew I had to get myself together, but I had not worked for thirty-five years, I had no formal further education, and we were in the middle of a recession. I was terrified and lonely. My youngest child was about to go away to college, and how many times a day could I walk the dog?

"I have always loved medicine and describe myself as 'a frustrated medical person.' I decided to volunteer at a Manhattan hospital. The manager at the volunteer services told me immediately that I was a 'people person' and that she knew exactly where to send me. What a boost to my nonexistent self-esteem! I was sent to fill in for a patient facilitator in the ambulatory surgery unit who was away on maternity leave. Three weeks later the manager of the unit asked me if I was looking for a 'real job.' The patient facilitator I was filling in for left to take another job, and I stepped into her role. I was the only new hire in the unit for many years and in fact am now the only facilitator in the unit.

"I cannot explain how all this has changed my life, how I think about myself, and how fulfilled I feel again to be needed and appreciated. My children will always be my first responsibility, but to know how proud they all are of me is the best feeling in the world!

"I have a wonderful support system, with my children and my friends urging me on. It wasn't always easy, especially as I had to get used to all the 'office politics,' but my new boss was always rooting for me, and now I feel just about one of the team, though not always, as most of the people I work with come from totally different lives than mine.

"Many years ago, back in London, I happened to meet one of the few successful women CEOs of the time at an extremely elegant party. I knew she had a husband and two children, and when we were introduced I asked how she did it all. She answered me with these words, which I have never forgotten: 'The only way that I can have it all is to accept the fact that nothing, and I mean nothing, in my life gets done properly.' I now know what she means!

"I don't believe in regrets, because I truly believe that at whatever point I made a decision, I thought it was the right one at the time. There's no point in berating myself for something I cannot change but learn from in the future.

"I will always be my children's mother. I am no longer my husband's wife, but now I have a new role in life. I am in a really good place right now. I have a demanding, rewarding, nine-to-five job and children who may not need me physically, but nonetheless need to know that I'm on the end of a telephone. There's also a wonderful new man in my life, who has also helped me reclaim myself. I have not been this happy for a very long time."

You go, Diana! Diana's story shows us it's never too late to try a new adventure. She could easily have thrown in the towel after her divorce, but she didn't. Instead, she reached out, volunteered, and found a new purpose in her life. From the tone of her story, it seems she's enjoying her life immensely, even if she's in a very different place than she thought she would be in. Sometimes life throws curve balls. Remember: You can't control everything. But just because your life starts to move off the path you planned, that doesn't mean you're moving on the wrong path. Instead, it could be that the right path was always there waiting for you, but you may have been too distracted by the wrong path to see it.

ASSEMBLE YOUR TEAM

After our amazing experience in New York, our show was sold to Kraft and SC Johnson for forty-two episodes. That is a huge order, especially for two moms who met in a Mommy & Me class! This was the time we had to dig deeper than we ever imagined if we were to fully realize our reinvention.

Now that we had forty-two episodes of a show to create, we had to set our pride aside and start calling on people we didn't even know. It was time to tap the village to get the right kind of help to make a successful show and also free up more of our time to spend with our families—which was a huge part of all of this to begin with!

STAY TRUE TO YOUR VISION

Once we started seeing all the options that were available to us, we both made a conscious decision that we were willing to make less money if it meant we could still be at pickup and drop-off. Remember, the idea of the reinvention is to have something for you, but still enjoy your family life. If your reinvention means you're being spread too thin, you're defeating its purpose. Keep that in mind when you're assembling your team.

As we write this book, we are having our own growing pains. Barb is on vacation in Hawaii with her family and is spending half of her day in the business center of the hotel, working. Jen is not only working while her kids are in school, which was the plan, but is now going right into her office as soon as the kids get home, which wasn't the plan, and her kids aren't happy about it. The lesson here is to remind yourself of two things: 1) Your reinvention, just like life, is a fluid situation. Adjustments have to be made throughout. 2) Remind yourself what the life you're trying to create looks like, and stay true to that vision.

GETTING BACK IN "THE GAME"

For those of you whose reinvention involves getting back in the workforce, Lori McInerney of Career Builder gave us some great advice: "If you're taking off three or four months versus four or five years, that's a big difference. There are a lot of tools out there to help you, and companies are definitely catering to working mothers more than ever. No one should ever be ashamed of taking time off from (her) career to be home with (her) children.

"There are lots of ways you can transfer your motherhood skills to skills in business. I have a lot of friends who were off for a few years and came back. They were head of the PTA; they had organized huge events. That is a lot of time management, that is project management, that is organizational skills, and that is a lot of stuff that you can transfer to business today.

"Online courses are great, whether (you're) learning things about Microsoft and Excel or different industries. (They) can help you get advanced in your own job, or for someone who has been out of work for years, this is great for them to take a look at how to get back on course for what (she is) going to need for (her) new job. You can do them at your own convenience. We actually have a lot of mothers (who) use our tools.

"One thing we have is Career Builders Salary. I think CB Salary is excellent for a lot of reasons. If you have been out of the workforce for awhile, you should get an idea, based on your skills and what you have been doing and your past experience, of what you are worth today."

This is an exciting time in your life. You now know love in a way you never thought possible. You have more responsibility than you ever thought reasonable. Take some time and pick a career that is going to fulfill you personally and fit your new life.

WHAT MAKES *YOU* TICK?

We shared with you how we were able to make our reinventions a reality: We found the thing that really spoke to us, got to the nut of what really made us "tick," and that's what made it happen for us. If we didn't feel so passionate about what we were doing, if it didn't cut to the core of who we are, we may not have had the will or the desire to keep it going. So it's not only important to find out what gets you going; you need to discover what's going to *keep* you going. You need to find what that one thing is that will make you get up every morning and you will want to do despite stumbling and rejection and not having validation in it right away. You want to find the thing you would be doing if nothing else mattered.

You may know exactly what this is right now, and you may need some help finding it. If you already know what drives you, great! If you don't, maybe even better. Now you have an amazing opportunity to tap into the person you've been living with your entire life and see her for who she is outside of everyone and everything else. You have a whole world of options open to explore. An amazing world of opportunity awaits!

How can you tap into what makes you tick? Do some research. Take the first thing that pops into your head and start reading up on it. There's a lot to be said for following through with ideas that seem to come out of nowhere. It's not that they come out of nowhere; it's that they come from your gut and intuition. They spring up without you thinking them through, and sometimes this makes them more you. You can make yourself think things that may not be accurate. You may think yourself into believing that you want to join a book club because a lot of your friends seem to enjoy it, but your gut doesn't lie. If you'd rather be playing an organized sport like soccer or basketball or ultimate Frisbee, you're going to feel restless in the book club.

All of this is okay, by the way. Discovery really is a process; eventually you'll get to the place where your brain and your gut agree, and you'll be able to move ahead. Enjoy the process of trying new things and playing out your ideas while you're at it. You're not being graded on this. It's all about you.

The Internet is your friend. It's an informational font you can tap into at three o'clock in the morning when you can't sleep and the library's closed. You have access to so much information. You get an idea and you Google it. "How long does it take to get a real estate license?" or "What kind of equipment do you need for rock climbing?"—whatever you want, it's all there.

Look to your village to explore your options, whether they're the people in your circle, the other mothers at your school or whom you've met at the playground, or your virtual circle. Talk to other women, other mothers, and see if there's something you can connect on. Pay attention to what people you know are tweeting or sharing in their Facebook statuses. Reach out to others in your own community, and see who comes back to you. You may find there are more people in the same boat than you realized. We found the woman who helped us with our theme song after Jen reconnected with her after twenty years on Facebook!

Reinvent Your Village: Social Networking Can Be More Than Social

You don't have to conquer the world in order to reinvent. It could be as simple as becoming president of the PTA—or even joining the PTA and attending regular meetings. If you haven't been getting out enough and crave the company of people in your situation, you're not going to find a situation with more people in the throes of motherhood than associations and events related to your kids' school.

Speaking of school, it's not just for your kids. If something intrigues you, investigate whether there's a class available. You don't have to spend a lot of money taking courses at your local college or committing to matriculating in a degree program. Investigate the continuing education options offered for adults at the high school or through your community center. For a couple of hundred dollars or less, you can explore screenwriting or fencing or pottery making or speaking Italian, and if you don't like it, next semester try something else. If you do, sign up for another class.

This is a process, one you should be enjoying. It's okay if you don't always follow through on what you do. Your time is limited, and your possibilities are infinite. You want to explore as many of them as you can. If something isn't working, it's okay, in this case, to leave it and move on to something that might.

MOTHER OF REINVENTION: LISA

LISA BAKER MORGAN, forty-one, divorced, two kids (ages nine and seven)

BEST ADVICE: *You do not have to be "perfect" at everything. We do not have to be career women, be PTA mothers, have perfect bodies, and have enviable social calendars. Our only obligation is to be the best person we can be, and that is to be defined by us only.*

"My reinvention came about when my husband and I separated. The unexpected change in my life gave me the push to do something I always loved to do and wanted to pursue, but had never had the courage to do.

"I love to cook, and I always have. Life was handing me my second chance, and I decided it was time to turn my longtime 'hobby' (as my then-husband referred to it) into a career. But I had to figure out how to pursue it in a way that permitted me to continue to be the mother I wanted to be. This was tricky, for several reasons. First, I had to figure out exactly what I wanted to do with my love of food and cooking. Second, I had to figure out how to do it around my mommy obligations. Third, I had to switch gears.

Before I became a mother, I was a lawyer, and all of my connections and contacts were in the legal field.

"I had a lot of practical experience cooking and planning events throughout the years. I started cooking when I was a child. My mother and grandmother taught me. I read cookbooks like novels. I started by focusing on event planning and catering-style jobs. I began a small catering service, which I named "ciao yummy!" (thanks to my children) and trademarked the name. I helped people with their children's parties. I volunteered to cook for or plan meals at various schools. I helped plan and provide food for church events. I donated dinners and cooking parties to charities for their fund-raisers. I gave out a lot of freebies, but I needed to build a reputation, even if it was in a small way, and every little bit helped. Word got around and led to other opportunities.

"Despite my practical experience, I always wanted to attend culinary school. My first choice, Le Cordon Bleu in Paris, eluded me. I could not pack up my children and move to Paris to attend school. However, they were finally in the same school, and I now had more than two hours to do something. One Thursday evening I unexpectedly discovered that a Le Cordon Blue program had begun in Hollywood, ten minutes from my home. A lightbulb went off. Everything fell into place within forty-eight hours. I found someone to drive the girls to the bus stop. My housekeeper agreed to come earlier, and I was set.

"I also developed relationships with local farmers and vendors as a result of the generous support of my professors. I petitioned the school to allow me to do a nontraditional externship and use my catering jobs and work on my book to count as my externship (as opposed to the traditional route of working in a restaurant, which was not compatible with my obligations to my children).

"One day I taught a friend to make something, and she said to me that she thought I should teach classes. The comment struck a chord. I did a few demonstrations, and later I began teaching classes in Los Angeles. I enjoyed the interaction and sharing with others the knowledge I had. Skills I had acquired as a lawyer enhanced my research and teaching style. I looked for part-time teaching opportunities in France and worked in Normandy in the summer of 2010 in a castle, where I taught tourists how to prepare classic Normandy dishes. The owner offered me a job as a visiting chef, and I will be returning in the summers to teach again.

"My former husband was not supportive in the least. He tried to use my attendance at school and my cooking as 'evidence' in court that I was not a devoted mother, that I was selfish for hiring someone to drive them to the bus stop in the morning while I was in school. He was critical of my company and poked fun at the name and my ambitions. His comments did not bother me. However, there was a morning at school where I spent a little too much time in the walk-in because my hollandaise kept breaking. I was tired and I just needed to cry a little in private even if it was freezing cold; the child custody trial on top of everything was emotionally draining.

"For the time being I have found the balance that works for me and my children. The truth is that I am fortunate to have a former husband who pays child support, which gives me the financial ability to take on my career at a pace suitable to motherhood. I am also fortunate that I have control over my schedule. I can take on as many teaching classes as I want, and I am able to choose which dinner or catering events I am comfortable doing. If there is a job that conflicts with an event the girls have, be it a play or a Brownies camp-out, I will not take the job. The last few months I have cut down on my class schedule to focus on writing, which I truly enjoy.

"I have no regrets about anything in my life. I am truly the happiest I have ever been, and the greatest thing for me is that I got to that place on my own, without being rescued by a man or looking to another marriage for security. Every experience I have had in my life has led me to becoming the person I am today, and the most painful experiences turned out to be the most positive. I am a better woman and a better mother as a result.

"Acceptance that some things are beyond my control has also brought personal growth and peace. Now I know that neither is there a guarantee of good days nor are there 'bad' days. Life is just a gift of days: Some go the way we like and expect, but others do not. The latter present us with opportunities to learn things we never knew we did not know, to meet people we now could not imagine life without, to experience joy in a way we might not have anticipated, and to recognize beauty in the everyday. Nothing is ever a waste of time, but an opportunity. Life will not allow you to be insincere; you will end up where you belong if you are open to it, and life will teach you if you are willing to learn."

It sounds like Lisa has been to hell and back with her divorce. Her reinvention fueled her to keep on going, and we are sure that having that piece for herself is what helped her get through what was surely an emotional rollercoaster. She is an inspiration.

GET TALKING

Who do you know? What are their strengths? How can they help you? Dig deep into your Rolodex, so to speak. Don't only consider who you know, think about who those contacts might know. Maybe your pediatrician's son's wife has something to offer. You never know until you start digging.

Calling on the friends and contacts you already have is the fastest and most efficient way to get you where you want and need to be. You just need to be able to put yourself out there. You need to be able to ask. The first call we needed to make may have been a daunting experience, but if we hadn't made the call, if we hadn't reached out as we did and broken out of our comfort zone, our reinventions would have never happened.

Reinvent Your Village:
Ask Questions—It Does Not Make You Look Stupid

You can start literally by looking in your own backyard, over the fence, and at your neighbors. Who are the people around you? You may be surprised to find the gems you have living around you, and how many of them may want to help you. As a good neighbor, there are probably ways you can help them, too. But you won't know until you reach out.

Now that you're on this path, you're also going to start talking to people with purpose and focus. It's going to be easier to discuss what you need and what you're looking for, because it will be a part of you. When we first got together, we talked about our kids. Then, as things started coming together, we started talking about our business idea. Now every time we talk to a mom, we try and decide if she can be on the show. Every conversation we have, we wonder if there's material somewhere in there. Don't discount the people around you as having nothing to offer. When you start looking at them through the light of reinvention, you'll see more possibilities than you ever imagined.

GET DOWN TO BUSINESS

One of the big obstacles people put in their own way is that they can't do what they want to do because they don't have the money to do it. That's not necessarily true. As we discussed previously, there are plenty of ways to explore your options that don't cost anything at all. There are others that don't cost very much. The problem lies in not using money as an excuse, especially when you might not need it to start making it—if that's what you want to do.

We each had $5,000 to put into our venture; maybe you don't have that luxury, but you can start getting creative in how you go about doing things.

MOTHER OF REINVENTION: FRANCINE

Double Effort, Double Reward!

FRANCINE LASALA, forty, married seven years, two kids (ages five and two)

BEST ADVICE: *No matter what seems to be holding you back, whether it's time or money or lack of support, the only thing ever truly standing in your way is you, because there's nothing else you can ever really control except your own intent and actions. Get yourself moving in the right direction, and miracles will happen.*

"I think like most women, I have reinvented in stages throughout my life. But the most significant one came when I became a mother. I had always wanted to be a mother. Even before I was married I had set up my career, as a freelance writer and editor, to be able to work from home when my children finally came along. But I think like a lot of women, I didn't have a realistic concept of what being a mother would mean, and how much my life would be affected by it—and this was both times. I was literally thrown for a loop with each child. I love my children with all my heart; I love being their mother, but because I was dissatisfied with other situations in my life, namely my professional life, I felt dissatisfied across the board; and it infected my happiness at home.

"Though I have always wanted to be a novelist and screenwriter, I've done mostly nonfiction—mostly ghostwriting other people's books. You don't generally get paid unless you actually sell a complete work of fiction or script, so I always worked where the money was and dabbled in the other world 'when I had time.' So I started writing *Rita Hayworth's Shoes* before I met my husband, and for many years all I had completed was the first two chapters. It was in the throes of motherhood that I realized I had to get it done. Especially after my second child came along, I felt like I was operating like a machine, completing mindless task after mindless task, and churning out books that had nothing to do with me. On top of that, the recession hit us hard. Scarily hard. Clients stopped paying me on time, and some stopped paying altogether. So I had to work twice as hard at a job I wasn't loving to make half the money, whenever it came in. It sucked. I internalized it all. I felt horrible about myself. I gained weight (thirty pounds *after giving birth*) and stopped caring about it.

"I knew I loved my husband and daughters, but I was frustrated and bored and just felt trapped in my life. I was a fat, frumpy machine, just going through the motions and making everyone around me miserable—when I saw other people. My husband works crazy hours and travels most of the week. I didn't see friends because I had no money to pay a babysitter or to go out. And I didn't want to see anyone anyway, because I had nothing to talk about except what a loser I thought I was. Between taking care of my children and house and trying to corral impossible finances, combined with soulless, 'pro bono' work, I had nothing for myself. My husband always encouraged me to go and find something for myself, but I always found a way to talk myself out of it because, of course, I had *no money* and *no time*.

"One Saturday morning I was ghostwriting a sex manual and also drafting a book proposal on personal finance, plus working on copy for some random catalog, making the kids breakfast, doing laundry, and getting the kids dressed for the day, when my husband came downstairs and told me he was thinking about going out to shoot some hoops. Something switched on in me, and I don't know what it was about that exact moment, but out of nowhere I said, "No. You can't. I'm taking a walk." I grabbed my iPod, slipped on a pair of flip-flops, and took off. I walked for half an hour, listening to my own music, feeling free for the first time in years. Then something remarkable clicked in my brain while I walked. I could feel the cobwebs starting to clear. It was as if I had just stumbled upon an attic. In that attic was a trunk called "Rita Hayworth's Shoes," which just popped open. Plotlines started racing through my head. Characters I hadn't thought about in years starting speaking to me. I finally found a place where I wanted to be, where I felt alive, and I realized I had to go there again and again. I was addicted.

"The next morning I got up at 5:30 a.m., put on a pair of sneakers, and walked again. Every day after that, I got up at 5:30 and walked more and more. My story started becoming more clear. Ideas were popping into my head that I had never before imagined. My awesome husband came home from work one night with a new pair of special sneakers for me, which came with a special chip I could sync to my iPod and track my progress. I started walking one mile a day, then two, then three. I started a Facebook group to get fans for a book that was only two chapters complete, and I kept walking and writing in my head. I've never been a good sleeper, and now, instead of spending the hours I was up in the night watching TV and worrying, I started writing.

"Within six weeks I had completed a draft and dropped twenty pounds. I felt great for the first time in years. I really began to enjoy my family more because of this. I enjoyed going out in the world again because I felt I was a worthy part of it. I was the woman who wrote the book about the magic shoes! I was someone aside from my husband's wife and my children's mother.

"Because I already had so much experience in book publishing and no track record or platform as a fiction writer, I decided to publish the book myself. I had already conquered the time obstacle by somehow finding time. I still had no money, so I had to get creative again. I set up a Facebook fund-raiser to cover the publishing costs, and I covered them all and then some. The support I had from people I knew and people I barely knew was amazing! I arranged a barter with another editor friend, who edited my manuscript for me. A designer friend was thrilled to design the cover for me in exchange for a night out. I didn't hire a proofreader: I ran a contest for free books to the first "fans" who responded and agreed to read the galleys for typos. I am still tapping friends in publicity and magazine publishing to try to get my story—about my story—out there, and though it takes more time than I ever could have imagined to do this, slowly but surely, I am doing it.

"This reinvention has been an incredibly rewarding experience, on many levels. Most important, because I am a better human being, more connected to my true self, I am a much better wife and mother. I am able to play with my kids and connect with my husband as the fun, happy person they deserve to be around, and that has made all the difference!"

Francine took resourcefulness to a new level. Not only did she rediscover her passion for writing what made her happy, she managed to incorporate that reinvention with losing the extra weight that had been bothering her. She had no money, and she found a weight-loss program that was essentially free. She needed money to publish her book, and she came by it creatively, getting a whole network of people behind her. The point of her story is that if you want something, you shouldn't allow anything to stand in your way. There are no excuses.

WHAT DO YOU WANT?

You can make your business as big or as small as you like. If you love making pies, you don't need to start a marketing campaign to start selling them. Start small. Reach out to your neighbors and the other families you may know through your kids' school. Get your legs under you and see if this is really something you want to do often enough to warrant making it a business, or if it's something you'd actually prefer to keep as a hobby, maybe making one pie a week for your family. Test the waters first before you devise a complicated business plan and head to the bank for a small business loan.

Reinvent Your Village: Test out Your Ideas on Your Neighbors

Even if you want to start a business and generate income, you may want to establish yourself at first by giving your services away. (This is a great test to see if you're really so passionate about what you're doing, you'd do it for free!) You know you make great invitations. People always compliment you on them, and you really love to make them. Is this the business for you? You may start by asking a couple girlfriends if you can do their invitations for free, and ask them to spread the word. You may not be making money, but you'll be collecting the tools you need to make money: referrals and material for your portfolio.

MOTHER OF REINVENTION: KERRI (PART 2)

Organizing the Chaos

KERRI HANCOCK WHIPPLE, married eighteen amazing years, three children (ages fifteen, thirteen, and eleven)

BEST ADVICE: *Throw your love for your passion out into the world and see where it goes. You just might end up exactly where you wanted to be.*

"I always struggled with 'wanting more' when my kids were young, and yet, at the back of my mind, feeling that home was where I needed to be during the season of my life with young children. The mental challenge was hard for me to not be stimulated and to have my day be filled with minutiae, and just have the next day, of MORE minutiae, to look forward to enduring.

"I would complain to my husband about wanting to look into doing something, but I could never come up with what that 'something' was. He encouraged me to do whatever I felt I needed to do to feel fulfilled. I think the idea of actually going out and following through with what I wanted terrified me. So the next best thing was to complain and just feel that I was trapped, even though the only one trapping me was myself and my fear. So the years tumbled along, and nothing was really done about that part of me that was searching for something more. In hindsight, I know that timing is a gift, and doors open at certain times for a reason.

"The occupation I wound up doing fell in my lap. I have always loved to organize things. Growing up, I would fill my time waiting for my sister to finish her horseback riding lessons by organizing my Mom's purse. I loved things tidy and manageable.

"Later in life I loved to organize my closet. Closets seem to have a life of their own with women, and soon, once I had seen a few friends' closets, I offered to help them with cleaning them out. Time flew for me when I was sitting with girlfriends in the middle of their closets, laughing hysterically about what was still in there and the stories behind the clothes. It was a great way to connect with friends and also help them with a strength I had that they didn't.

"This eventually led me to start an organizing business. A friend of mine was moving, and I offered to come and help her get organized and go through all of her stuff to see what needed to be purged and what needed to be packed. She loved how much I was helping her, yet felt bad for taking advantage of my offer in friendship, so she wanted to pay me to continue to come and help her. She asked me what I would charge, and I was completely confused about how to answer this question. I had never been paid to do this for anyone. We agreed on some number, and I came back and helped her finish her home. This was the beginning of a grassroots business for me. Word spread, I had clients, and my business began. I couldn't believe it.

"My husband was very supportive, and my children thought it was cool to say that I had my own business. My hours never really infringed on their day, so it worked out very well for us as a family.

"I thought I wanted to go back to work and just 'get out of the house,' but in reality, I wanted to use a strength I had, get the feeling of accomplishing a job, and feel appreciated for the work I completed. These are needs that are not always met when dealing with young children.

"If you are thinking about beginning a new path, look at what you are naturally good at and do not assume everyone has the same talents. These are special to just you, and you should share them, even for free in the beginning. A lot of times how you live your life is the greatest advertisement for yourself. People watch other people and will admire you for the special talents you have if you showcase them in your life. If you are always dressed well and love fashion, a friend might ask you to go shopping with her to help with her style. If you are good at flowers and love flower arranging, offer to help with a school event's centerpieces. If you are great at throwing your kids birthday parties, a friend might ask you to help with a party she is throwing.

"You don't have to start out huge and take a huge risk. Start small and learn along the way. Build your confidence and don't ever feel you are not good enough or ask, 'Who do I think I am to ever think I could actually get paid to do what I love?'"

Kerri was stuck for a long time. She found her reinvention in something that she loved and that she was good at. Sometimes we need to just look in the mirror to see what is looking right back at us.

REINVENT WITH A FRIEND

You can reinvent by yourself or with someone else. Sometimes it takes a village; sometimes it just takes a special person whose contribution to your reinvention is worth the weight of an entire village! Sometimes you need both—and sometimes you don't need either. Reinvention is different for everyone, after all!

If having a partner appeals to you, it doesn't necessarily have to be another woman or even a mother, although it helps when the person you're relying on is going through just what you're going through. Whether it's someone to walk around the block with you three times a week or someone to start a business with you, using the "buddy system" will help motivate and inspire you. Buddying up helps get you moving, and it takes away the isolation.

Reinvent Your Village:
Try the "Buddy System"

We have two friends who were struggling with fitting in a workout. They hired a yoga instructor to come to their homes to teach a private class for just the two of them. Now they both have to show up, or there is no class. It's been a great motivator for them.

Having a "buddy" also takes the pressure off. Especially if you're starting a business, it not only helps to have two people doing the work, but you also have someone to be accountable to. We rely on each other; if one of us misses a deadline, we both have to readjust to set things right again.

It's a good idea to pick someone who has strengths that you don't have. Say you love baking but hate accounting. Great! Find a numbers person to pair up with. You get to be in charge of making the pies—and your partner gets to be in charge of making the pie charts!

Barb used to run a marketing company, and in our endeavor, she handles the business end and crunches the numbers. Jen is more creative, and she's the one who helps us articulate our ideas. Even when we're in production, Barb likes to do the editing, while Jen writes the voiceovers and the outlines.

Buddy up with someone who brings something to the table that you're lacking. That way you can divide and conquer. Having each other helps us get out of our own way, and because we handle different aspects, we also get out of each other's way.

If your reinvention does involve another person, whether as a business partner or an exercise buddy, that's another relationship that in and of itself needs continued reinvention. As you grow into your reinventions together, you will notice changes in one another. Just as in a marriage, it's not always easy, but the strength of your relationship relies on being able to grow together.

Barb

In the beginning, Jen used to have her husband come in on our calls, and it would really upset me. She used to lean on her husband a lot more. She felt her husband's opinion was more valuable than hers, and that really got to me. I'd say things to her like "Jen, I don't care what your husband says. You're my partner. Whether he has good advice or not is not the point. This is about you and me together and making this happen. Whether we succeed or fail, it's about you and me." We had two or three arguments over this in the beginning, but we have come around. We've kept our respect for one another and created something really special here and, like a marriage, we don't want to ruin it by bickering.

As long as I'm giving 100 percent, I feel good about things. If you feel something isn't going your way or you're not doing something right, ask yourself if you're giving 100 percent. Even in arguments I've had with Jen, I get off the phone and ask myself, "Did I give my 100 percent? Was I being fair? Was I not being sensitive or understanding?" I want this to work, so I make sure I do everything in my power to make it work.

Jen

There is no way that I could have done this without Barb. I love creating; coming up with ideas, and writing. I do not, however, enjoy dealing with the money and the numbers. It is not that I don't want to know about it, but things like taxes and contracts are just not my cup of tea. Barb, on the other hand, loves it. I mean loves. You should see her when she gets her calculator out. It's like someone gave a kid an ice cream sundae! I also don't know if I would have been nearly as motivated if I didn't have someone to do this with. We cheer each other on, we are dear friends, and we always manage to pick the other one up when one is down. I cannot say enough about having a "buddy."

We've been at this for awhile, but not without troubles along the way. At one point we had to fire an editor. But we also had our share of struggles within our partnerships—with our husbands, as we pointed out, when it came to airing our dirty laundry—but also with each other. You have to work at your reinvention, just like your marriage. But when you share a reinvention with someone else, when you build something like this with someone else, it can be twice as rewarding.

TIME CAN BE MONEY—BUT THAT DOESN'T MEAN MONEY WASTED

We can't say this too many times: Reinvention takes time. Nothing happens overnight. You need to stay patient and grounded and experience and learn from each part of your reinvention as it's happening. Take baby steps, and you're less likely to tumble and fall.

There was a silent auction at Jen's kids' school, and one of the prizes to bid on was a private meeting with Mark Burnett (the creator of *Survivor*). Jen won, and for $250, clinched a fifteen-minute meeting with him for us. We ended up spending more than an hour with him.

We explained that we weren't trying to pitch a show, but we were looking for advice on our show, which, though not necessarily a "reality" show, had a very "real" edge about it. He really liked our idea and believed we were onto something. He gave us this advice: "Don't run before you can walk. Keep putting along until you have it down. You're only going to get one shot on TV, so make sure you're ready."

That really stopped us in our tracks. We were so determined that TV was the next step for us. We had been going gangbusters, and we realized after that meeting that we didn't want to put the cart before the horse and risk everything. We stayed intense and passionate and dedicated, but we slowed down a bit after that meeting to make sure we really had all the pieces in place and that we were really ready before we put ourselves and our show out there.

We talked about our idea for a year before even getting started. And once we set our plan in motion, it took another whole year to get paid. But we kept at it, slow and steady, and we learned a lot along the way.

Don't get sidetracked by details. If you can't figure something out right away, don't get stuck there. Go try to figure out something else and then come back to it. That's a big reason why people stop. They want everything to fall into place in a logical succession, but it isn't going to happen that way. If you get hung up, you're going to wear away at your self-confidence, and that's going to be a debilitating obstacle. Control what you can control and let go of what you can't. Don't let one minor roadblock prevent you from moving forward; walk around it and come back to it later.

They say that time is money, but that's not really true. If you rush through without all your ducks in a row, "saving" time is going to cost you later.

WORK IT OUT

Reinvention is work, but it's work worth doing. It will make you a happier person, and as a result, everyone in your family will be happier. This is a big deal, and that means it will be a big deal as it's unfolding. You will get in your own way. Others will get in your way. You will doubt yourself, and others will doubt you. In fact, even for this book, we were told we weren't ready to do a book and that we really didn't have a marketable concept. We didn't listen. Just like everyone else, we got rejected, but we kept going.

We were flirting with the idea of signing with one of the biggest Hollywood agencies. We were working with them, but hadn't signed anything yet. We had written up a book proposal. It wasn't *The Mothers of Reinvention*, but it was in the mom space. We had a call with this agent in New York who was supposed to be on our team. It was like someone sticking a pin in our beautiful new balloon. She told us that we had a bad idea, that we weren't ready to write a book, that until we had a regular spot on a national show we wouldn't be ready, and that there was no place in the market for it. When we told her that we had been scouring the bookstores and there was nothing like it out there, she told us that was probably for a good reason. Let us remind you that she was on OUR team!

You have to keep going. We know you can do this. When a door gets slammed in your face, go through the back door. If that door shuts on you, open a window. If the window's locked, find another way. If you want it badly enough, you can make it happen. You just have to want it badly enough.

Remember: Having kids does not mean the end of opportunity in your life. It's an opportunity to look at opportunity in a whole new light. Invest in yourself. Out of this will come a more fulfilled person, a better wife, and a better mother.

NOW YOU KNOW

Reinvention involves you and your family, but it also reaches beyond your house, into your backyard, and into your "village." Here are some of the main points we covered in this chapter:

- You have to keep your eye on "the big picture." It's not the hiccups you encounter each day, it's the small steps in spite of them that get you closer to where you need to be.
- You have to be creative with what you have available—and that goes for time, money, and all other resources.
- You have to be brave enough to ask questions—to open up to others, let them know what you're doing, and see if they or anyone they know can help you.
- Take your time. There is no deadline here. Really think about what you're doing, *feel* what you're doing, each step of the way. The only way you waste time is to force yourself to move ahead more quickly then you need to—and end up back at the starting gate all over again.

Chapter 5

Reinvent *You*
Your Ten-Step Guide to Loving Your Life!

I was sitting in my hotel room in New York waiting for my family to arrive. I had been there for four days working, and I missed them so much. I couldn't believe Jen and I had won a Webby, the Internet version of an Emmy. It seems like yesterday I was crying in my bathroom, so depressed, praying to God to show me my purpose in life, to give me strength to be a good mom and survive.

Back then I was feeling so ungrateful, so guilty about everything, seeing no happiness in sight. Yet here I was three years later, happy, fulfilled, with purpose, and my family was totally with me. I remember my first job I got out of college, my boss said to me that it was easy to be successful in business, but it was very hard to be successful in both your business and personal family life. I see how proud my daughters and husband are of me, and I feel fulfilled. It is through this journey with my family and my friend Jen that I found the path to my reinvention.

—*Barb*

I recently celebrated my ten-year wedding anniversary. Jonas told me if he had to give a grade to our marriage, it would be a hard-earned A.

He said that's the best kind of A, because it didn't come easily. We really had to work on it. He surprised me with an intimate dinner for two, hosted at a friend's house, prepared by a professional chef. It was the most romantic thing anyone has ever done for me.

As we were talking about our journey together, he told me that since I had been doing *Mom Life*, he has seen wonderful changes and growth in me and that it has made our marriage and family better. We both had tears in our eyes.

I feel justified in my dreams and at peace in my life. I want to bottle this feeling and be able to take a little swig from it every time I feel a little down.

—Jen

Through reading this book you should now know the following things: 1) why you aren't happy, 2) that you need to adjust your expectations, 3) that your family is not the problem, 4) that there are more support and resources available to you than you may have realized, and 5) that you are not alone! You've come around to seeing that feeling unfulfilled as a person in your role as wife and mother is within your control to fix and change.

REINVENT YOU: NO EXCUSES!

This is the chapter at which you stop wallowing about the things that aren't working, start taking action, and set your reinvention in motion! It will be easy to find excuses daily to not reinvent. That we can assure you; we've been there. Ask yourself now: What's stopping me? Whether you want to sign up for a cooking club or join a gym, or take some business classes offered by a local continuing ed program or get a college degree, not necessarily in something that will help you advance professionally, but in something that excites and fuels you, something that you're passionate about, what's stopping you?

It's time to get out of your own way. Because you're not only doing this for yourself, you're doing it for your family. You want to be a good role model for your kids, so show them you're a person who's ready to grab life by the horns and follow your dreams. Tell yourself what you tell your children, to follow their dreams. You can be anything you want to be. You cheerlead for your family daily—start cheerleading for yourself as well.

Jen

When we first pitched our show to the company that we now partner with, they passed on it. It was a really big letdown. This meant that we were not going to get the money to film the sizzle reel (imagine a collage of what the show would look like). We knew we needed that to interest any sponsors. Instead of throwing in the proverbial towel, we decided to shoot it ourselves. I armed my husband with a camera, and Barb and I started filming. Luckily, while we were still filming we got the eleventh-hour call that the company was interested and going to give us some money! I'm glad that we didn't quit. We were determined to do it ourselves if we had to.

Barb

Jen and I had just committed to each other to do our web series when my husband lost his biggest account at work and could possibly also be losing his business.

I was in shock. We had just planned our finances so that we could do without my income for a year, the time I needed to start this new venture with Jen. There was no way we could survive without his income, too. What was I going to do? Did I have to give up my dream? I was already forty, and if I was going to make a change, this was my moment. I was at a crossroads. Did I just go back to my old job?

Then inspiration struck. Just like that I thought, we could rent our house and move into a smaller space. Renting out the house would provide the extra money I needed to keep my dream alive.

That was a drastic move, but that's how serious I was about my reinvention. I needed this reinvention to happen. This was not some luxury. It was a necessity for my survival and for my mental health. In comparison, moving was a small price to pay, and it ended up to be a fun adventure for my whole family.

We set this up as a ten-step plan. Don't let that stress you out. You don't have to enforce a timeline on your reinvention, but you do need steps to act on it. As we and the other mothers of reinvention you've met in this book have told you throughout, reinvention takes time. It would be impossible to quantify this for everyone, as everyone's reinvention happens at its own pace. So don't feel confined by these steps as a schedule. Instead, use them as a roadmap for the steps you need to take. Cross off things you've been able to address and view them as daily victories. Each of these daily victories will help fuel you to continue on your path to reinvention.

FUEL YOUR PASSION

We've learned so much from our journeys that the success we have found is a side aspect of it. We've grown exponentially as human beings. We're excited to get out of bed in the morning for two reasons: the love of our families and us having our own slice of the pie. The passion from having our own piece of the pie fuels everything else. We've found the *pep in our step* that was lying dormant for awhile.

We have both reinvented, just like the other mothers we've featured in this book, and we, just like them, are continuing to reinvent every day. The moments we shared with you above—Barb's excitement about having her family join her in New York for a few days, Jen's amazing celebration of a marriage grown so strong after really working at it for ten years—are a couple of the poignant moments we experienced when we knew our reinventions were working. We can't wait for you to enjoy moments like these and many more as you work to become the happy, fulfilled woman, wife, and mother you deserve to be!

Jen

I had a voice, and I needed it to be heard. I definitely rocked the boat at home, but I had to do it. It was a necessity for me. I was willing to take my marriage to the edge because I felt so passionate about it. I did it to fuel my passion. My husband lives with a different woman, and for the better.

I feel like every part of me is alive and working on a high level. I feel alive and awake in a way I never did before. I'm at an age when I realize that life is hard, but that doesn't mean it's bad. I have the important things. I'm intellectually stimulated in a way I've never been; I feel excited to get up each morning not only because I have a family but because I'm excited about what I'm doing. It makes me look forward to the future. It reminds me that anything is possible.

NOW YOU KNOW

Reinvention is within your grasp, and you are going to feel more alive with every passing day. You discovered that having a dream isn't enough: You need a plan, and you need to follow the plan. You now have the tools you need to set your reinvention in motion. So what are you waiting for? If you still have doubts or are not convinced how necessary this reinvention is to you and your family, take a look at what our husbands have to say.

SHAHRAD, ON BARB

My wife, Barbara, has always been extremely positive, with a great happy energy about her. More than anything, she has loved and drawn great confidence from her work. But as our kids got older, her passion and love for her business was no longer there. Her work, which had always been a great source of confidence and energy for her, was now draining and exhausting her. The girl who could flash her big smile in any situation was around less and less.

So Barbara made the brave choice to start the reinvention journey. I was scared and excited for her as she started this journey into the unknown. This journey of reinvention has not only brought her full circle to the person I met in the summer of 1997, it has gone beyond that. She has a newfound confidence, not only about herself, but also about our family and our marriage. It is a confidence that I have never seen before. She jumps out of bed in excitement for her work. At this point, I can't even call it work, because she loves what she does. I have fallen in love with her all over again.

JONAS, ON JEN

As Jen's husband, I've had a front row seat at her reinvention. I have to admit I'm not all that surprised. Jen has always had a knack for balancing the ever-changing cycles of life; her inherent wisdom is one of the reasons I fell for her.

After we had Cooper, she claimed that she wanted to go back to work, but I didn't really believe it, so when she got pregnant with Lilah five months later, it wasn't surprising that she wanted to be a stay-at-home mom. She was truly focused on being the best possible mom to our kids, but I could sense that as our kids got older, she wanted to do something beyond motherhood. We would sit in bed at night and talk about what the attributes of the "perfect job" might be. We made lots of lists. She wanted to do something that would keep her inspired but not interfere with motherhood. There were false leads, late-night fits, lots of soul searching. When she hit on the idea of a talk show for moms, it seemed like a great but daunting idea. Who would pay for it? Would it work? Would it interfere with play dates?

You have to show up in life and go out and risk something in order to succeed, and that's exactly what Jen did. She showed up, asked questions, worked hard. She'd get knocked down and then pick herself up again. She utilized whatever resources she had at hand. As I've watched her business grow over the last few years, Jen has still remained a mom in the truest sense. For Jen, that IS success. She's proud of herself. And so am I.

TEN-STEP GUIDE TO JUMP-STARTING YOUR REINVENTION

It all comes down to this: ten steps as a plan of attack for you to get your reinvention in order. This schedule's function is to help keep you structured in your awareness that you need to make time for yourself every day.

Even if it's just a matter of taking a fifteen-minute walk, you have to do it. Who knows—that fifteen minutes of walking could lead to an hour of walking. That walking could lead to running. That running could lead to signing up for a marathon someday. You don't have to dive right in. You can dip your toes and test the water. You just have to start taking baby steps toward having something for yourself. For making time for yourself. For giving yourself a sense of accomplishment that you can only get working toward something that's yours.

Step 1: See the Signs

You know you love your family, but something isn't working. You feel a void, a sense of unrest, of there needing to be more for you somehow in your life—but what?

When something seems "wrong" to you, write it down. If something doesn't sit right, no matter how petty or strange or un-related it feels, make a note of it. If you feel like you're losing pa-tience too quickly, write down the things that are making you nuts. Don't overthink this. If your child's asking you a question every forty-five seconds and it is driving you off the deep end, write that down. If you've walked into yet another open drawer because your husband hasn't quite grasped the concept of "clos-ing," write that down. Don't judge yourself and tell yourself you're being petty. Don't second-guess yourself and not include these things. The point is to be as open and honest with yourself as possible. It's an important first step to becoming open and honest with your family and anyone else you're going to need to rely on to make your reinvention a success.

Next, write down the things that do seem to work. When do you find that moment of peace, of joy? Is it being able to shave your legs in the shower on a weekday? Have you been able to look through a magazine that entertained you while you waited in the car for your child to finish up soccer practice? Did you con-nect with another human being in line at the bank? Whatever it was, however small, write it down.

See if there are any patterns emerging in the notes you've taken. What are your biggest frustration triggers—and who's trig-gering them? How many of these things you've recorded are signif-icant, and which may seem trivial on the surface, but are perhaps symptomatic of something else? What about the joys? Was there any one thing that came up again and again? Which section has more entries?

Unless you know what you're dealing with, you can't fix it. Isolating these challenges or frustrations is the first step to moving past them.

Step 2: Find Your Passion

You've taken the time to consider what's working in your life and what isn't. You have a book of notes to refer to that makes the pros and the cons of your life instantly accessible. You now have a "study guide" to refer to as you turn your attention on yourself. Now is the time to write down what you love to do. What are you passionate about?

You have our questionnaire in Chapter 2, and you can also download it as a PDF at www.jenandbarb.com. We can't stress enough how important it is that you do not rush through it. Go back to it often as you work through your reinvention and really think about what you need to feel more fulfilled in your life. A writing class? A new business? This is how you figure it out.

Enjoy this process. Don't worry about figuring everything out and changing things immediately. The fact that you are taking the time right now is wonderful.

Step 3: Make the Time

This is how you start to figure out how you're going to fit in what you love to do! Pay special attention to your responses in the "Hours I Devote"/"Hours I Want to Devote" columns in the questionnaire. Compare non-mom you to mom you. Really look at the two of you. What do you want for yourself? How much time are you spending doing the things you love? And how much more would you like to add to that?

Record all the tasks you do this week and how much time it takes you to complete said tasks. Divide the pages into columns if that helps: Tasks/Time. Include everything from waking up the kids (and whatever you're doing before at the crack of dawn, like balancing your checkbook or making cupcakes for the school bake sale), to whatever goes into getting them out the door and to school—and everything you do if they're still home with you, to everything you do from play dates to numerous activities, to dinner, bath time, bedtime, and everything you do between their bedtime and yours. (And if you or your kids are not good sleepers and you get up in the middle of the night to do things, you're going to have to record those things, too.) At the end of the week, add up all the time.

Yes, this is tedious as hell. But it's going to help you in two ways: 1) You'll be able to see what the time suckers are ("Did I really devote three hours this week to driving other people's kids around?") and 2) you'll be able to see at a glance what really needs to be done by you. Do you have to prepare a meal every night? Could you get some help around the house so you don't have to devote hours to cleaning bathrooms? As we told you in chapter 2, you don't have to do everything yourself. Look at these tasks and mark up which ones can be done by someone else and which can be eliminated completely.

Here's the other thing you're going to do. You're going to try to say "no" five times a day. Make a checkmark in your journal each time. When you can comfortably get to five marks, see if you can increase that number. It may seem like a lot, but it won't when you see an inventory on paper of everything you say "yes" to.

Step 4: Strategize

Saying no is of course only going to get you so far, when you say no to 15 requests and yes to 253 others. For those things that have to be dealt with, that you can't farm out or eliminate, figure out how to delegate within your house.

Before you approach the people you live with about any task you think should be theirs, plot out your strategy. You are the general, and these are your troops. Who's going to be most effective in which way?

Step 5: Get Your Spouse on Board (If You Have One)

How is your relationship with your spouse? Are you living in a war zone? Are you ready to turn things around?

Are you pissed off about razor stubble in the sink again? If you take a deep breath, can you try to not scream about it? Have you come home to a child whose diaper hasn't been changed in so long, it's dragging on the floor? Or school-aged kids loading up on junk food and watching TV instead of doing their homework and getting ready for dinner? If you take a deep breath and don't otherwise open your mouth, can you deal with the situation rationally—even humorously (and by humorously, we do not mean sarcastically). Instead of finding fault with everything your partner is doing, appreciate the effort. Instead of thinking about how to phrase your next gripe in a language he will understand, think about how to turn it around.

Yes, you may be dealing with sloppiness and filth and later-than-usual bedtimes, but look around: Is there something, anything your partner did right in the same period of what you perceive as slacking off to purposely make you nuts? Okay, so the pizza was burned, but did he at least try to make dinner? Try to refocus on these things instead. Who knows, you may actually find this is a nicer way to live.

Also compare what you may expect from your partner with what he might actually be able to deliver. What are your expectations, and what are your *realistic* expectations? Remember, you want to set up your spouse to succeed. It's important to understand this, because it's time to break down that ginormous task list, and the more realistically you figure out what he can and cannot get done, the less frustrated you're going to be when he can't meet your expectations.

Now make the list or chart together of who can realistically do what and when. You'll also be able to communicate and bounce ideas off each other about what the rest of the troops can do.

And guess what? You're halfway there!

Barb

I'm doing what I want on my own terms. I've chosen what I want to do—what I would do for free. I asked myself what would fulfill me and went for it. I'm completely inspired and excited about the journey of this reinvention. I have wanted to be a talk show host since I was a little girl. My reinvention is dessert. I put all the other important pieces in place first, and I've enhanced everything with that one thing that's for me. I was looking for my own piece of the pie, and now I have it. I'm so happy to be at an age where I can actually appreciate it. If I had been on the same journey at twenty-five, I wouldn't have appreciated it like I do now.

Purpose is such an important part of a person's existence. To identify your mission and work toward it is everything. I feel that Jen and I have navigated being able to work and get this little piece for ourselves. We've found what works for us. We've created our own existence. We've navigated family life with a little piece for ourselves front and center—and I am a much better person, mother, and wife because of it.

Step 6: Get Your Kids on Board

Now that you and your partner have gone through what needs to be done and what each of you can humanly do, decide what your kids can do. Write down what you think your kids are able to handle. Knowing their personalities better than anyone else in the world, you know what you can realistically expect from them and how to get results.

The other side of the reinvention with your kids mirrors that of you and your partner. If you're taking time away that they perceive is their time, you have to address how to handle that with them. Again, consider each child separately—their needs and individual personalities. Maybe one of your kids has a hard time separating—even if he or she is older, he or she still likes having Mommy around more than not. List the benefits they'll get from Mommy being happy and fulfilled. One child might respond better to being able to spend more time with a beloved sitter, while another may be excited at the prospect of getting involved in whatever you're doing (we talked about the cupcakes and being a cupcake tester in chapter 3).

By the end of this step, you should have some grasp on how to help your kids accept that you can be both "Mommy" and "You."

Step 7: State Your Claim

From now on, this is what you are. Not "what I am going to be." Switch "I want to be" with "I am." Remember: Perception is reality. If you believe it, others will believe it, and they'll respect you for it.

Step 8: Reach Out Now

So you want to learn how to play guitar. So you want to start a business baking pies, or you're writing a novel and need an editor to look it over. This is when you look very specifically at the people in your backyard and work to expand your community. Have conversations with people, and see if they know other people who could help you. Your community consists of everything from your mommy friends to your friends on Facebook. Your job at this point is to gather as much information about your interest or passion as possible. Remember, have no fear! If someone judges you, that is her problem, not yours. You really have to reach out of your comfort zone here. Do it!

Step 9: Try, Try Again!

This is the time to see if the "hat" you have chosen fits. You may find that stylish fedora you chose looks good, but when you go to the beach, you're still getting sunburned. The good news is that you know you need a hat. Okay, this one didn't work. Trust us, you'll be in a better position for finding the one that does. You just may have to try on a few.

Step 10: You're on Your Way!

Now that you've made tweaks and adjustments and gotten everything running just the way you need it to, you can finally be on your way. You're still going to have to keep working at it, but at least now you have a firm blueprint in place to guide you and to change and adapt, as your life, and you, will surely do.

This is it, ladies. We have opportunities like never before. The women before us have made it possible for us to have choices. Let's honor them and ourselves and take action. When you start to reinvent, you will feel very good about yourself, and that good feeling will affect everyone you come into contact with—especially your family. Now is the time!

And remember, we're all in this together.

Meet Your New Village

Renee Avedon married her high school sweetheart, and when their two children were born, raising them became her top priority. After her son and daughter became old enough to not need her full time, she decided to pursue a new career that would allow her to indulge her love of houses and people. Her passion fueled her choice, and in just her first year in the business she achieved sales of over $10 million. She involves her children when she regularly raises funds for her favorite charity, People Assisting The Homeless (PATH), and for other causes. "I believe it's important for us to teach children how lucky they are to live in a nice home and have so much," says Renee, "and I do that by exposing them to organizations helping people who have very little." rbavedon@aol.com

Pam Caulk Bacich is the mother of two amazing adult children and grandmother of six. A native Californian, she's a graduate of the University of Washington and feels lucky today to live on the water in Newport Beach, California. Pam can be found boating from Mexico to Alaska five months of the year and is a passionate photographer. Her recent shows include "Nets and Buoys" at the Newport Nautical Museum and "Abandoned Dreams" at Anne's Wine Shop. Pam is currently working on a photography book about the Day of the Dead in Mexico. www.pambacichphotography.com

Diana Lynn Barnes, Psy.D., is an internationally recognized expert on the assessment and treatment of perinatal mood disorders. She is the co-author of *The Journey to Parenthood: Myths, Reality and What Really Matters*. A past president of Postpartum Support International, she currently sits on the President's Advisory Council for that organization. She is also a member of the Los Angeles County Perinatal Mental Health Task Force. In addition to her private practice, which focuses on women's mental health, Dr. Barnes is a nationally known forensic expert in women's reproductive mental health and regularly consults with defense counsel on cases of infanticide, pregnancy denial, neonaticide, and child abuse. Dr. Barnes is a fellow of the American Psychotherapy Association and a clinical member of Postpartum Support International, the American Association of Marriage and Family Therapists, and the California Association of Marriage and Family Therapists. She is the 2009 recipient of the Welcome Back Lifetime Achievement Award from Eli Lilly for her courage and achievement in the depression community. dlbarnes@post partumhealth.com

Elaine Bauer-Brooks is a happy wife, proud mother of two, and most recently the founder/editor of the losangeLIST, a neighborhood guide and lifestyle website based in Los Angeles. She was the head of development for the Style Network, having created such shows as *Kimora: Life in the Fab Lane* and *Ruby*. While she was serving as vice president of development at Imagine Television, *24*'s "Jack Bauer" was named after her (and the uncle of the show's executive producer). Elaine@thelistcollective .com; www.thelistcollective.com

Lauren Booth is an artist and mother of four who currently resides in the countryside in Connecticut. After living abroad for sixteen years, thirteen of them in London, in 2010 she and her husband decided to reboot their lives to be closer to nature. When not doing homework or cheering for her children from the sidelines, Booth can be found working at her studio among the trees. Booth has had her sculptures and neon artworks in several group shows and has had two solo shows of her work in London. She is also the creator of The Illumination Show, a body of neon artworks for which world leaders, including the Dalai Lama, Bono, President Clinton, Thich Nhat Hanh, and Oprah, have written inspiring thoughts. Her most recent projects include bronze door hardware inspired by her recent move and laser-cut steel outdoor lights. www.lauren-booth.com; www.theilluminationshow.com

Betsy Brown Braun, M.A., is a child development and behavior specialist, a parent educator, and a multiple birth parenting specialist. She has taught in both public and private schools, has been a school director, and was the founding director of Wilshire Boulevard Temple's Early Childhood Center in Los Angeles. Betsy consults with parents privately and runs parenting groups, seminars, and workshops for parents, teachers, and other professionals. She is the award-winning author of the best-selling *Just Tell Me What to Say: Sensible Tips and Scripts for Perplexed Parents* and *You're Not the Boss of Me: Brat Proofing Your 4 to 12 Year Old Child,* both in their fourth printings. Betsy has been featured on the *Today* show, *The Early Show, Good Morning America Now, Dr. Phil, The Rachael Ray Show,* and *Fox and Friends,* and has been a guest on NPR and radio stations nationwide. She is also a contributor to *Parents Magazine, Twins Magazine, Family Circle, Good Housekeeping,* and numerous city-specific newspapers and family magazines. Betsy and Ray Braun are the parents of adult triplets. www.betsybrownbraun.com; betsy@parentingpathways.com

Melissa Burnett is a native Californian who was raised in Orange County. She has a BA in psychology and enjoys travel, horses, skiing, and spending time with her family above all else. She lives in Los Angeles with her husband of eight years and their daughter, Alexis. www.thepaci-fairy.com

Stephanie Davis began her entertainment career in the William Morris mailroom, after attending New York University's Tisch School of the Arts, Cardozo School of Law, and being admitted to both the New York and California Bar Associations. She went on to work at Addis/Wechsler, Artist Management Group, and 3 Arts Entertainment, and now runs her own management/production company, Wetdog Entertainment. Film and TV credits include *The Extra Man*, USA's *The Starter Wife*, Lifetime's *Maneater*, and HBO's *Bored to Death*, currently wrapping its third season. She lives in Los Angeles with her two children, Alizee and Oliver.

Anne Tracy Emerson is an Emmy award–winning network television producer and writer with twenty years of experience in the investigative news and documentary field. Her career includes time spent overseas as the associate bureau producer for ABC News-Johannesburg during South Africa's transition to democracy. She went on to become a producer for ABC News and The Discovery Channel in the United States, where she won an Emmy award for her series documenting the trouble in our oceans. Anne has since crisscrossed the country as a freelance field producer for most of the major network and cable channels, reporting on a variety of stories. In addition to her work in journalism, Anne is also a founding partner of Kids' Yoga Journey, a Charleston, South Carolina–based company that integrates family well-being with current technology. Kids' Yoga Journey (www.kidsyogajourney.com) created the first yoga iPad application designed specifically for children, now distributed across several digital platforms, including the NOOK color for Barnes & Noble. Anne graduated from the University of North Carolina at Chapel Hill with a BA in journalism and mass communication. She lives in Charleston with her wonderful British husband, Patrick, who still thinks she looks good in a bikini, and her two kids, Luke and Lily, the stars in her crown.

Before having two children, **Kabrel Geller-Polak** was the owner of The Geller Agency, a boutique Below the Line talent agency in Los Angeles. She represented many Oscar- and Emmy-winning cinematographers, production designers, editors, costume designers, and first assistant directors for film and television. Prior to owning her own agency she worked at various talent agencies, learning how to juggle itineraries and organize and plan meetings, schedules and vacations, and day-to-day operations of an agency. Many of these skills are necessary to being CEO of Annabelle and Emet, her two children. Most recently she became involved in a new restaurant/bar/entertainment venue, Vodvil.

Becky Beaupre Gillespie is an award-winning journalist and the coauthor of *Good Enough Is the New Perfect: Finding Happiness and Success in Modern Motherhood* (Harlequin Nonfiction, 2011). She is a former newspaper reporter who has written for the *Chicago Sun-Times, The Detroit News, USA Today,* and the *Democrat and Chronicle* of Rochester, New York. She and her *Good Enough Is the New Perfect* coauthor, Hollee Schwartz Temple, have spoken on motherhood, perfectionism, and work/life balance to audiences and media outlets nationwide, most recently appearing on *MSNBC Live.* Together they write the work/life balance column for the *ABA Journal* and blog about parenting and work/life balance at TheNewPerfect.com. A recovering perfectionist who is happiest creating her own (ever-evolving) fit between work and family, Becky lives in Chicago with her husband, Pete, an employment litigator, and their two daughters. becky@thenewperfect.com.

Lisa Borgnes Giramonti is a domestic explorer who examines modern life through an Old World lens. The topics she is interested in include style, travel, food, literature, gardens, eccentrics and their foibles, and whatever else makes her gasp for breath. www.abloomsburylife.blogspot .com; lborgnes@mac.com

Dr. Michelle Golland is in private practice as a clinical psychologist in Los Angeles, California, with a focus on issues relating to couples and individuals. She is also an expert in multicultural and community psychology. Dr. Golland is a national media psychologist and relationship expert and has appeared on *Dr. Drew, The Situation Room with Wolf Blitzer, Larry King*

Live, *Campbell Brown*, *The O'Reilly Factor*, HLN, ABC, NBC, *Access Hollywood*, *The Insider*, *Extra*, and many more. The media turn to Dr. Golland when they need an expert opinion on psychological issues related to anything in popular media. This year alone she has appeared in the national media over a hundred times. She is also an expert and contributing writer on the popular website for mothers, Momlogic.com. Dr. Golland has also been quoted in *People*, *US Weekly*, and *OK* magazine on a variety of topics. Her blog, "Musings on Marriage, Motherhood and Madness," is filled with her signature writing style of sharing her own vulnerabilities and failings in a way that makes her real to those who seek her guidance. www .drmichellegolland.com; info@DrMichelleGolland.com

Risa Green is the author of two critically acclaimed adult novels, *Notes from the Underbelly* and *Tales from the Crib*, which were the basis for the 2007–2008 ABC television series *Notes from the Underbelly*. In 2010 Risa made her young adult debut with the novel *The Secret Society of the Pink Crystal Ball*. She also writes a popular weekly blog called "Tales from the Mommy Track" on HYPERLINK (www.mommytracked.com). Prior to becoming a writer and mother of two, Risa worked as a high school college counselor and also spent two years doing hard time as a corporate attorney. Born in the Philadelphia area, Risa now lives in Los Angeles and somehow squeezes in a few hours of writing each day between morning and afternoon carpool runs.

Mahtab Mossanen Hakim was born in Iran. She and her family moved to the United States in 1979, and she has lived in Los Angeles for thirty-two years. Mahtab was a schoolteacher for three years until she had kids of her own, Lola (age nine) and Sacha (age four). She has been married to Afshin Hakim for more than twelve years. When Lola turned one, Mahtab began the journey of her new career as the owner of Wonderland, a children's boutique in Brentwood. Aside from running the store, Mahtab enjoys spending time with her family, cooking, reading, and being very much involved with her children's schools. www.childrenswonderland.com; childrenswonderland@msn.com

Francine LaSala is a freelance writer and editor who has written, ghost-written, or collaborated on more than fifty works of nonfiction. She has also written several feature-length screenplays and recently published her first novel, *Rita Hayworth's Shoes*. She lives in New York with her husband and two daughters. www.francinelasala.com

Diana Levitt was born in London, England, and moved to New York City in 1997. The proud mother of five children, she is divorced and lives in Manhattan, where she works in health care at a major New York hospital.

Dr. Wendy Mogel is an internationally acclaimed clinical psychologist and author of the *New York Times* best-selling parenting book, *The Blessing of a Skinned Knee*. A popular keynote speaker, she lectures widely at conferences and schools. Her new book, *The Blessing of a B Minus*, is available now online and at local bookstores. www.wendymogel.com

When the ten-year relationship with her former husband ended, **Lisa Baker Morgan** made lemonade out of lemons and used the change as an opportunity to follow her passion for cooking while at the same time maintaining her commitment to motherhood and her two young daughters. Formerly a litigator in a large Los Angeles law firm, she used her prior restaurant and event-planning experience and turned her "hobby" into a business, creating a catering business, ciao yummy !® She later attended Le Cordon Bleu College of Culinary Arts in Los Angeles, graduating with honors. Currently she is a private chef in Los Angeles and also teaches cooking classes in Los Angeles and France. In 2010 she began a successful blog (www.chefmorgan.com) and is currently working on a book. In her "spare time," Chef Morgan runs two to three marathons a year and continues to be actively involved in her children's lives, whether she is coaching their soccer teams or leading their Brownie Girl Scout troop.

Shelly Naphtal is a psychologist and life counselor who encourages positive, compassionate, and solution-oriented thinking. Shelly integrates clear intentions, compassionate forgiveness, and release of judgments with focused action steps to resolve conflicts. Her approach incorporates gratitude, grace, and humility while assisting her clients in accessing personal strengths, core values, and inner resources. She assists in providing a framework for replacing negative thoughts with positive, self-honoring choices. Every challenge becomes an opportunity for learning and growth. Shelly's commitment to maintaining a positive attitude supports living life while managing situations rather than living situations and managing life. Today Shelly enjoys a life filled with love, meaning, happiness, and joy, which she shares with her loving husband and three children. With a BA in philosophy and an MA in spiritual psychology, her professional life includes a private practice, women's groups, parenting workshops, corporate seminars, and public speaking engagements. shellynaphtal@hotmail.com

Candice Pate is a creative, team-oriented executive with extensive experience in brand building and new media. She recently worked as chief marketing officer for the Sun Valley Marketing Alliance, a destination marketing organization charged with bringing more visitors to Sun Valley, Idaho. Before she took a four-year break to raise her young children, Candice was an integral part of the team that launched the Hallmark Channel, Hallmark Cards' first 24/7 cable network. Prior to Hallmark, her experience included work in new media and television marketing and production, including producing shows for VH1's hit series *Behind the Music*. Giving back to the community is very important to Candice, and she has served as a leader on a number of boards, including as president of Harvard-Westlake School Alumni Board and vice chair of Sustain Blaine, Sun Valley's economic development organization. Candice has a BA in politics from Princeton University, where she earned Academic All-Ivy status as captain of the volleyball team. She lives in Sun Valley with her husband and two children.

Linda Perlman was born in Miami, Florida, and currently lives in Los Angeles. She attended the University of Miami and taught nursery school. Now divorced after a twenty-four-year marriage, she is a stay-at-home mom with three children, ranging in ages from seven to nineteen.

Connie Tamaddon has worked in photography and video production for more than ten years and is the founder of i-design, a children's photography business. Her work has been displayed in galleries and schools and has been published in various newspapers. She has filmed and edited fund-raising videos for various nonprofit foundations, including *The College Track, Global Fund for Women, One Hen,* and *Pets in Need.* She lives in Menlo Park, California, with her husband and two children. www.surprisingsilhouettes.com; www.connietamaddon.com

Dr. Bonnie Eaker Weil (Dr. Bonnie) is a relationship expert who was named by *Psychology Today* as one of America's best therapists and by *New York Magazine* as one of New York City's best therapists. Known as "The Adultery Buster" and the "No. 1 Love Expert," she is the bestselling author of *Adultery: The Forgivable Sin* (adapted into a Lifetime movie starring actress Kate Jackson); *Make Up Don't Break Up, Finding and Keeping Love for Singles and Couples* (rev. ed. 2010, including DVD *How to Fall in Love and Stay in Love for Singles and Couples*); *Staying Not Straying, How Not to (S)mother Your Man and Keep a Woman Happy; Financial Infidelity (Making Money Sexy)*; and the winner of the *New York Times'* Reader's Choice award for best dating book 2010 for *Can We Cure and Forgive Adultery?* Dr. Bonnie has appeared on ABC's *Good Morning America,* in a three-day series on NBC's *Today* show, on *The Oprah Winfrey Show,* in a four-day series on Fox TV about dating, in the Discovery Health documentary *Infidelity,* and on A&E's *Addictions.* She appears frequently on ABC, Fox, CBS, and NBC News, *The View, 20/20,* and CNN. www.DoctorBonnie.com.

Kerri Hancock Whipple grew up in Phoenix, Arizona, and attended the University of Southern California. She graduated with an education and English degree in 1990. After graduating she lived in Newport Beach, California. She married Jeff Whipple in 1993, and they have three children, Hailey (age fifteen), Matt (age thirteen), and Amy (age eleven). The family moved to Phoenix, Arizona, in 2000, where Kerri began SOS: Sort. Organize. Simplify. They moved to Park City, Utah, in 2009 for an adventure and are still there enjoying the mountains! Kerri currently is a mentor mom for Mothers of Preschoolers (MOPS); is involved in missions and local outreach organizations; and enjoys book clubs, bible study, entertaining, and hiking with girlfriends. Whipplekerri@gmail.com

Book Club Questions

Was motherhood what you expected?

How are you managing your life? Do you feel it is out of whack? If so, in what way?

What are you passionate about? What would you do for free?

What does your perfect life look like? Be specific.

Fill out the questionnaire on page 62. Hand your questionnaires around to the group. One at a time, go around the room and discuss the responses. Each person should comment on what she sees emerging.

Set up goals for the group. For example, in two weeks we will all do _____, or by next month my goal is _____. Check in with each other to see if you accomplished your goals. If not, talk about what your obstacles were.

About the Authors

Jennifer Pate was raised in Highland Park, Illinois. She attended the University of Illinois at Chicago while performing in theater and dance in Chicago. After years of traveling the world and performing, she moved to Los Angeles and became a casting director for film and television, cofounding Colloff, Fishman and Britt (CFB) Casting. Jen switched gears again after having her first child, to become a stay-at-home-mom for the first five years of both her kids' lives. She now is the cocreator and cohost of *Jen and Barb: Mom Life*. She lives in Los Angeles with her husband, Jonas, and their two children, Cooper and Lilah.

Barbara Machen was raised by a single mother on government assistance in a suburb called Daly City (population 100,000), outside of San Francisco. One of a dozen kids in a graduating class of five hundred to receive a full scholarship, she attended USC. She owned a marketing company for fifteen years. She is currently the cocreator and cohost of *Jen and Barb: Mom Life*, she lives in Los Angeles with her husband, Shahrad, and twin daughters, India and Soraya.

Please contact us at info@jenandbarbmomlife.com and visit us online at www.jenandbarb.com.